To the C

Please return
to the rack when you
are through.

Reck

JUST OFF THE GROUND

Recollections of an Aviator

CARL "RECK" RECKNAGEL

FITHIAN PRESS ■ SANTA BARBARA ■ 1993

Book design by Eric Larson

Published by FITHIAN PRESS
A division of Daniel and Daniel, Publishers, Inc.
Post Office Box 1525
Santa Barbara, CA 93102

LIBRARY OF CONGRESS CATALOGING-IN-PUBLICATION DATA:
    Recknagel, Carl
        Just off the ground : recollections of an aviator
            p.   cm.
        ISBN 1-56474-067-6
        1. Recknagel, Carl.   2. Air pilots—United States—Biography
        TL540.R337A3   1993
        629.13'092—dc20
            [B]   93-13492
                                                                CIP

Contents

List of Illustrations

Foreword

TO ANYONE who has long been retired I strongly recommend writing a book about some small piece of history in which he may have been involved. I can promise that it will be a rewarding experience to start probing around in the back corners of one's memories. The recollections may not always be accurate, for time sometimes alters the dimensions of distant events. A two-pound trout caught in earlier days could well turn into a five-pound specimen thirty years later. But the experience of recalling and recording one's memories will certainly be gratifying, even though the book may never become a best-seller.

—CARL "RECK" RECKNAGEL

Acknowledgments

I OWE A DEBT OF GRATITUDE TO the many people who have contributed to this effort.

My daughter and two granddaughters got me started and kept me going with with their inspiration along the way. Emily Cox, the youngest granddaughter, wrote an inspiring biography of her grandpa while she was in high school. Lisa Forbes, my older granddaughter, who is a professional writer, has helped me put together this writing in many professional ways.

As for the photographs, most of the originals are crusty and old, but thanks to my friend Boz LaMere, a professional photographer, they have turned out reasonably well. Boz also contributed a lot of information about publishing such things.

JUST OFF THE GROUND

Introduction

SOME PEOPLE, MAYBE A LOT of people, including myself get an urge to write a book at some time or other in their lives. They may feel that their stay on this planet has been so full of exciting and unusual events that the world would be enthralled by an account of some of the history surrounding their own lives. I was encouraged to do this very thing by such folks as Ralph Lee, my closest and best friend during my formative years, by my daughter Margaret Cox and by my two granddaughters, Lisa McKenzie and Emily Cox.

At no time in my life have I ever been considered a poet or classical writer such as the great poet-writer Antoine de Saint-Exupery, who had not only the gift of words but also an adventurous background in the 1930s. His book, *Wind, Sand and Stars*, was considered a classic and is a reading "must" for many literary students.

I've read Saint-Exupery's book, but I can't relate to his wording of some of his great adventures in the air and on the ground. On his air combat missions he carried along an ink-bottle and a fountain pen to take notes of his encounters—a real feat.

A description by this author of a line of thunderstorms might go something like this: "The squall has ceased to be a cause of my complaint. The magic of the craft has opened for me a world in which I shall confront within two hours the black dragons and the crowned crests of a coma of blue lightnings, and then when night has fallen I, delivered, shall read my course in the stars."

I have a simpler outlook in my treatment of such a situation. In my crude way I would have described this lousy affair as a thunderbuster full of lightning, hail and turbulence straight

15

ahead, so detour around it or get your eyeballs knocked off and your gizzards shaken out. So I could never be a Shakespearian scribe nor compete with any of the classical folks, but that's O.K. with me.

So I will write a few chapters not only about my own past but about some behind-the-scenes events of early aviation in the Army Air Corps days and some beginning airline happenings.

My own lineage as researched and compiled by my daughter, includes a bit about a relative who was a horse thief convicted and hanged at sunrise the next morning. That would have made a good story had that reprobate kept notes or even a diary.

I will not attempt to compete with some of my favorite writers, among whom are Ernie Gann, Chuck Yeager, Beryl Markham, Ernest Hemingway, Margaret Eaton and others of that stripe. These authors have had great adventures and have a knack for talking to the reader in such a way as to give the impression that he is having a conversation with them, not just reading words out of a book. And the simplest of events come out as epics.

EIGHT decades out of any era bring changes so numerous that it would take a pretty sharp historian with an advanced computer to list them all, and would require more paper than exists today—and there's already too much paper.

Early on my mother kept a daily log containing shopping lists, cooking recipes, household expenses and bank deposits. Since my dad was paid in cash, the deposits represent what was left over after the bills were paid. I give here a few pages for the year 1907 as an example of how things have changed.

Travel habits of both babies and adults have also changed considerably. When I was months old my range of travel extended to the nearby grocery story in a baby buggy; whereas my new great-grandson Nicholas Forbes has, at age five months, flown from California to New York and return and shortly after to Australia and back home. Both of my granddaughters, Lisa and Emily, traveled around the world while in their twenties.

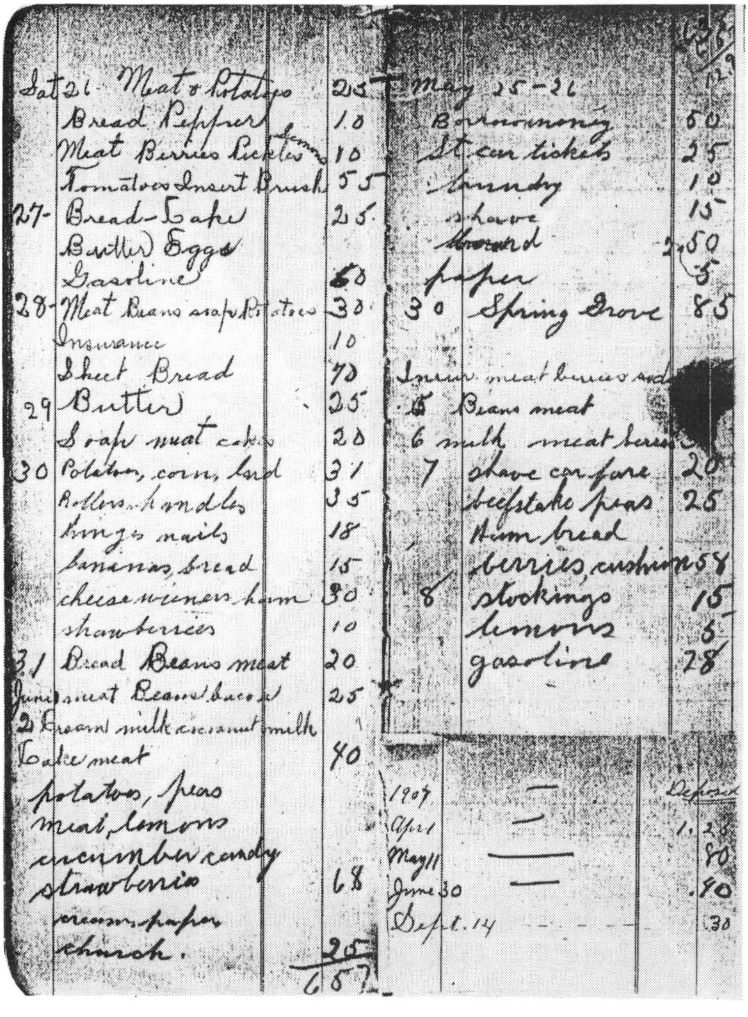

Sat 26	Meat & Potatoes	25
	Bread Pepper	10
	Meat Berries Pickles	10
	Tomatoes Insect Brush	55
27-	Bread-Cake	25
	Butter Eggs	
	Gasoline	60
28-	Meat Beans soap Potatoes	30
	Insurance	10
	Sheet Bread	70
29	Butter	25
	Soap meat cakes	20
30	Potatoes, corn, lard	37
	Rollers handles	35
	hinges nails	18
	bananas, bread	15
	cheese wieners ham	30
	strawberries	10
31	Bread Beans meat	20
June	meat Beans bacon	25
2	Cream milk cocoanut milk	
	Cake meat	40
	potatoes, peas	
	meat, lemons	
	cucumber candy	
	strawberries	68
	cream, paper	
	church	25
		657

May 25-31		
	[illegible]	50
	St car tickets	25
	laundry	10
	shave	15
	Board	2.50
	paper	5
30	Spring Grove	85
	Insur. meat beans [illegible]	
5	Beans meat	
6	milk meat beans	
7	shave car fare	20
	beefsteak peas	25
	Ham bread	
	berries, cushion	58
8	stockings	15
	lemons	5
	gasoline	28

	Deposit
1907	
April	1.23
May 11	.80
June 30	.40
Dept. 14	.30

My mother's household bookkeeping, 1907.

The aging process tends to remove one from the mainstream of life. It doesn't take much to illustrate this observation. In earlier days the letters H.S. meant horse sense—or use your head, it's not that complicated. Or you might even think like a horse, and I quote Lee Marvin of Hollywood, who said, "A horse is 1,500 pounds of untrustworthy stupidity that would prefer to knock your brains out under a low tree limb than to take you where you want to go. On second thought, if you were a horse would that be so stupid?"

But lately I've noticed that the phrase "horse sense" seems to have disappeared from our vocabulary. The initials H.S. now appear to relate to certain waste matter created by a horse's natural process of elimination. But don't get the wrong idea; flowers and plants prosper when given large doses of this product of a horse, cow, or even a chicken.

PHILOSOPHY

My oldest and best friend, Ralph Lee, probably shaped my philosophy of life as much as anyone, after my mother and dad got through with me. Ralph was the head of public relations for General Motors in Detroit. He had a working relationship with such kings of the automobile and aviation industries as Boss Kettering, Bill Stout and Orville and Wilbur Wright—all pioneers in their respective fields. I was introduced to each of these VIPs at one time or another. Ralph worked as a lad for the Wright Brothers during their early experiments and introduced me to Orville at the Engineer's Club in Dayton, Ohio. At the time I was a young, bushy-tailed second lieutenant fresh out of the Army Air Corps, trying to impress people with my boots and britches and especially with my wings; so when I met the Big Man my part of the conversation consisted mostly of opening my mouth without much coming out. However I did manage to blurt out that Ralph and I had just landed a Kinner Bird on the side of a hill near Mansfield, Ohio, because of a swallowed valve. Mr. Wright then asked me, "What, are you still swallowing valves?"

At the time of his death some fifteen years later, Orville

Wright would have been surprised to learn that I swallowed my last valve on a DC-7 airliner on a coast-to-coast flight. We didn't land on the side of a hill, but we did return to Denver to continue the flight with a new plane. While we lived at Dayton we made several attempts to lure Mr. Wright into taking a flight with us in one of our planes, but he always declined without giving a reason. Then one day veteran Benny Howard came by with a brand new four-engine DC-4, the largest airplane built to date, and he finally accepted.

Ralph didn't really have an office at General Motors, even though he rated a top-notch one. He preferred to do his thing in the field, giving talks around the country on many topics. For whatever reason he adopted me as a young upstart whom he would assist in tackling life.

I attended some of Ralph's roving talks, one of which related to etchings. For the talk he used a roll of toilet paper to illustrate his theme. The T.P. was used to wipe off the excess ink from the etched plate. The audience lapped it up. This great fellow was from the ground up.

Ralph's main hobbies included sipping a schooner or two of the bubbly stuff now and then, mostly every evening. I had the pleasure of his company on many such occasions, including one in Chicago when we had a contest to determine who could consume the most beer without leaving the table. At the end of nine glasses each we both left the table by mutual consent for some temporary relief, and the match resulted in a draw.

Ralph's other hobby was a home workshop, and he had the best. It included a complete woodworking and metal fabricating complex of machinery as well as a foundry. In a few hours one evening he demonstrated to me how to make an aluminum skillet from scratch. A wooden form of a skillet was made, a mold was formed, and the molten aluminum from the foundry was poured. After it cooled it was polished, and I had a shiny new skillet to take home to my wife. I've always had some kind of hobby shop, which may be attributed to Ralph's influence.

CHAPTER 1
Starting Out

DURING WORLD WAR I airplane activity was relatively heavy around my hometown of Springfield, Ohio, and consisted mostly of war planes from the nearby Dayton aerodromes. The sound of an aircraft overhead immediately drew everyone's attention, and they stopped whatever they were doing to peer into the sky. A plane in flight was a novel and thrilling sight at that time, but there were tragedies also. Decades later, people who live near airports mostly complain about the noise they make.

Once a combination carnival, zoo and aerial flight show came to town, bringing with it an early airplane made of bamboo with linen-covered wings. As the biplane was towed past our house en route to the carnival site, the mere sight of this ethereal bird thrilled me down to my toes.

Then I watched a balloonist jump from about two hundred feet up. His parachute didn't open, and he dug a hole in the ground a few feet deep and bounced as well. Many of the passing aircraft crashed either in or around our town. One flew overhead heading southeast and dipping low. I followed the machine and watched it plunge into a house, the skipper dead. Another flew over with his motor sputtering and went in. I followed the craft and found the pilot walking along a row of trees on his way into town, holding onto his severed ear. His partner was lifeless in the wreckage.

Numerous such incidents should have discouraged me from any further interest in aviating, but they only seemed to confirm an idea in the back of my mind that some day in some way I was going to become one of those guys who wear wings.

*

WHILE in high school in 1924, I saved enough money to purchase my first airplane ride. A barn-storming Jenny appeared at a dirt field north of town, the pilot offering rides for five dollars a throw. When I told my mother about my plan she said, "Be sure to leave your new pocket watch at home." I climbed into the cockpit and we started out bouncing over the rough field for takeoff. The engine quit cold, and after some cussing the pilot jumped out and grabbed the propeller to restart the engine. Sitting alone in the cockpit I fantasized that I was a real bird man until the pilot climbed back in and off we went. Circling around the area convinced me that this stuff was for me.

At home on Western Avenue, my mother forced me to practice music on the piano each day and to take lessons once a week, when actually I wanted to go out and build airplanes or do some empty-lot football—anything but poke a piano. I recall discharging a wooden spool filled with gun powder in the basement and her distress since she was sitting directly overhead, also her irritation when I removed the receiver from the telephone and hooked it up to the new crystal receiver I had built with my old friend Dick Lesh. The phone rang *sans* receiver. When my mother went to answer it she found an alarm clock holding down the receiver hook, the receiver being a block away. Looking back it appears that she had to endure a lot because of her son's chemical, radio, and aviation fiddling around.

Building a crystal radio receiver and having it work was a real achievement. It consisted of a galena crystal, a cat's whisker, a variable control with wires wound around a cardboard oatmeal box, and some sort of receiver—like one pulled off the nearest telephone. A Cincinnati station WLW came in well; but the real prize was the Havana, Cuba, station that came in every Saturday Night. "*Tick, tick, tick…*This is Habana, Cooba." Even with this early start with radios, electronics have always been something of a mystery to me. My solution to most electronic problems is a ball peen hammer: just tap it gently and it might work.

Many chemical experiments were going on in the attic of the

Curtiss Jenny, 1924, first time JUST OFF THE GROUND.
"Leave your new watch at home."

old homestead in Springfield. I tried myrrh, an old mystic substance that was an important product of trade in the ancient Middle East. It was used mostly to make incense, and was also used by fire-eaters to enable them to swallow flames. It was a gray, chewing gum-like substance, and I applied it to my finger for the heat test. I applied the flame and it worked just like it was supposed to; but in a few minutes the stuff began to heat up and my finger got scorched. Not only that, it also took a long time to remove the evil stuff.

Then came the mercuric fulminate job, a powerful explosive, easily set off by a slight jolt. I mixed enough of this compound to completely eliminate the city of Springfield, but it didn't work like it was supposed to.

My craving for chemistry, flying and general tinkering was partly satisfied by enrolling in the University of Cincinnati, College of Engineering and Science, with an eye to at least becoming a chemical engineer. The course involved 113 different subjects, three semesters a year for five years. Every other month we attended classes from eight o'clock a.m. to five o'clock p.m., and during the alternate months we worked at nearby firms on jobs pertaining to our chosen fields. My work assignments included soap manufacture, laboratory control of special soaps and what to do when a two-story kettle of soap boils over. I also learned that one should never walk around on a floor that is covered with lye solution. I tried this one day and got a large chunk of my foot burned off.

Other work assignments included instructing a class in metallurgy and metallography at the university and being a control chemist for an electroplating firm of Springfield. After a year of teaching the metallurgy and metallography course I knew as much about the subjects as the students I taught. At the firm in Springfield auto bumpers for Chrysler, Chevrolet, and Packard cars were electroplated. There I built a fine laboratory with the latest equipment, and the lab must have been a success, because I was loaned to the Packard Motor Company in Detroit to assist them in setting up an electroplating system for their radiators.

This last venture extended my range of travel many times over, including my first overnight stay in a fancy hotel in Detroit—most mind-boggling, since my campout days I had spent in a tent on Mad River near Springfield. I could now be classed as a world traveler.

One low point during some chemical experiments I was conducting occurred when I flooded the entire plant with a large dose of hydrogen sulfide, which smells just like rotten eggs. The president of the company came charging out of his office and demanded to know what the hell was going on. But in spite of this I was offered a fine job with the company when I graduated.

The curriculum at the university included joining up as an enlisted man in the ROTC program. Part of this training was an assignment to the Lunken Airport Air Corps Reserve unit, where my duties were washing, refueling and filling the radiators of the PT-1 planes and riding with some World War I aces on their practice flights around Cincinnati. Lieutenants Campbell and Winslow were among these pilots and were the two first aces after the United States enetered the skirmish.

My first ride with this staunch outfit was in a PT-1 with one of the aces. Just before this initiation the other lads in the unit fed me a large helping of strawberry shortcake. The flight was something else. For two and a half hours we spent most of the time upside down, and only now and then right-side up. I became violently ill and transferred the shortcake from my stomach into my flight jacket. As we wended our way over the hills around Cincinnati the engine started to hiss and cough and threatened to give out entirely. We returned to the field with a lad who had just experienced his first and last bout of sickness in the air.

Commencement day at the university, when I was to receive my award as a chemical engineer, was a notable occasion for me. Before my dad left Springfield for the ceremony he called me and said that there was a telegram for me from the War Department, and did I want him to read it to me. The message read:

"YOU ARE ORDERED TO REPORT TO MARCH FIELD CALIFORNIA WITHIN SIX DAYS AS A FLYING CADET OF THE ARMY AIR CORPS."

That was the first and last day of my career as a chemical engineer and from here on out the sky would be my playground. Since that day I have spent the equivalent of three years in the cockpit of an airplane of some type or other.

CHAPTER 2

Reaching the Goal

THE THREE-DAY TRAIN RIDE to California gave me plenty of time to make a plan, namely that this was for me and I would bust a gut to finish the course. About 1,200 civilians had applied for entrance to the academy, but only 144 had been appointed. Due to wash-outs and fatal crashes the graduates who flew in the commencement day events at the advance school at Kelly Field, Texas, would number only 44, and I was lucky enough to be one of them.

The arrival at Riverside won't soon be forgotten. Four of us early arrivals were greeted by an upperclassman named Charlie Thompson, who gave us a taste of the discipline about to come. Already the rigors of being a green plebe made us feel akin to a wooden plank.

Our little squadron of four was marching down the hangar line lugging our bags when a formation of planes roared over-head, minus two of its aircraft. Sirens started screeching, ambulances and crash wagons dashed around, and pandemonium reigned. It seems that an instructor and a cadet had just collided and both had been killed. Charlie snarled, "The first man that looks around will be sent home."

Some thirty years later Charlie died when an automobile he was unloading from a trailer rolled back over him. This must have been the first time his exercise of discipline ever deserted him.

After seven hours of flight instruction under Lieutenant Pop Weddington and a lot of ground school, my instructor decided that he had had enough of me and that henceforth I would be on my own. On my takeoff many thoughts crowded my mind in ad-

27

dition to the Lieutenant's instructions on how not to hurt myself. With computer-like efficiency I remembered some of them.

This first solo flight was supposed to be a simple circling of the field and a landing. As in any other business or profession, you must start somewhere. Immediately after takeoff I encountered my first hazard, one of many which would follow.

A dust devil appeared in my path, and a fast decision had to be made. I had never seen such a thing before, and I didn't even know what it was. The whirling monster of dust really mystified me. Would it destroy my aircraft and plunge me to the ground? My old philosophy about hitting your head with a hammer paid off, and I decided to fly around it; let someone else find out about these things. This required an extra circling of the field, and after I landed the instructor came up and growled, "I thought I was going to have to shoot you down."

While practicing landings one day near Riverside my motor sputtered and tried to quit. I looked around for a spot to set her down in and sighted a likely looking field and headed that way. But when I throttled back for the landing the engine kept putting out a little power, just enough to keep me rolling along the ground, too fast to stop within the field I had selected. I rolled over a ditch, wiping out the landing gear and almost ending upside down. Had my flying experience been a little more advanced I would have simply cut off the ignition switch and all would have been well.

Aerial maneuvers such as slow rolls, snap rolls, loops, falling leaves, and whipstalls were part of the curriculum. I disliked slow rolls and any upside-down flying because dust from the cockpit floor kept getting into your eyes. Nevertheless I became proficient in some of these but not up to snuff in others. My favorite maneuver was the whipstall, where the plane is pulled straight up to a dead stop then sliding backward tail first after which the plane toppled over to resume flying attitude. During the backward slide the controls are reversed. However one of my whipstalls turned into an upside-down flat spin, which is a bear to recover from. Luck was with me on that one, since I didn't know what to do, so the plane righted itself without further incident.

We advanced to more sophisticated machines like the DeHaviland-4 and the Douglas-02, both powered by the Liberty engine. Our first night flights were made in the Douglas, another important stepping stone. I've never found anyone who can adequately describe a pilot's first night flight in pitch darkness, probably because true darkness is so difficult to put into words. Some say that black is the absence of light, but what about the occasional twinkle of a light or two? It's like that classic old photo of a black cat in a coal bin: the eyes have it, but where does the cat end and the coal begin? The reliable old ploys one used to keep the plane right-side up are missing. Periods of downright awe are never over once one takes to the sky.

Crosscountry flights around Southern California were next on the program. These involved a blend of map reading, identifying objects on the ground, and the use of a magnetic compass. Compasses were never accurate in those days; a north reading could just as well mean that you were heading east.

On one such crosscountry on the road to Palm Springs in a DH-4, I was persuaded by the devil in me to enjoy my first roaring dive on some moving object, which turned out to be a truck tooling along the lonely desert road. I peeled off and commenced the thrilling maneuver, leveling off just above the top of the truck and climbing steeply, only to have the motor conk out. This ended my thrill of thrills; fortunately the motor started again seconds later, but the experience postponed any further dives for quite a while.

Upon graduating from March Field the class made its way to Kelly Field near San Antonio, Texas, for the final honing of our flying skills and training to become officers and gentlemen in the Army Air Corps. I made this leg of the journey in a venerable old Oldsmobile touring car with a couple of other cadets.

I drew attack aviation as my part in the new Air Corps, and my instructor was Lieutenant Lester Maitland, one of the greats. He and Lieutenant Hegenberger had flown a Fokker tri-motor plane from the U.S. to Hawaii, another first. He told me that when they thought they should be over the islands they had seen nothing but empty ocean. They turned around and saw the lights of Honolulu and realized they had overshot their destination. While in San Antonio Lt. Maitland also ran a cartoon series for the local paper and later became a minister in Red Bluff, California.

Our graduation ceremony from Kelly Field was held in June 1930 and had a number of firsts. One was the first troop carrier maneuver that was to evolve into the great troop carrier part in the World War II invasion of Normandy. A flight of planes flew over and dropped machine guns and small cannons by parachute; this was followed by troops who raced to the artillery and began firing.

As part of the two-day graduation ceremony our entire class of attack, bomber, observation and pursuit planes flew in review for the dedication of Randolph field, the new Air Corps training base. I flew the lead plane of the Attack Group, and I was probably put there so that the rest of the team could keep an eye on me.

After graduation, which my mother and dad watched, I was told that I looked pretty snazzy in my boots and britches and silver wings. At that time I had acquired a new 1930 Ford Roadster in which I and another second lieutenant, Jim Going, made our way from our alma mater to our first assignment, the Third Attack Group based in Galveston, Texas. This aviation seemed to be getting more exciting all the time.

Above: Lieutenant Jim Bevans.
Below: Old No. 263 PT-3, my solo plane.

Above: Lt. Irv Woodring and his class.
Below: After seven hours in the air I busted one without much damage to the aircraft but a lot to my ego.

*Above: University of Cincinnati graduates who
met for the first time at March Field (l–r):
Carl Recknagel, Cornelius Dunbar, Mike Hunt, Francis Jacobs.
Below: March Field plane lineup of PT-3 and DH-4 trainers.*

*Above: Cadet Mason in a PT-3 lands on Lt. Cumberpath and
Cadet Langelois in a DH-4. Many of these confrontations
occurred during our stay at March Field.
Below: Checked out on the DH-4.*

Above: Lt. Lester Maitland, attack instructor for my group. He
and Lt. Hegenberger flew a three-engine Fokker to Honolulu.
Later he became a Baptist minister in Red Bluff, California.
Below: Maitland's class (l–r):
Louis Waite, Bill White, Orville Oakes, and Carl Recknagel.

Above: Randolph Field layout before being completed.
Below: Typical low-level attack formation.

Los Angeles Airport Terminal (Mines Field), 1929.

Low-level attack formation, Kelly Field, Texas. Lead plane flown by the author. (Photo: 22nd Photo Section, Kelly Field, Texas.)

CHAPTER 3

Third Attack Group

UPON ARRIVAL AT GALVESTON I was assigned to the 90th Attack Squadron, commanded by Captain Virgil Hines, a WWI vet. My first job was as mess officer of the group. My experience as a gourmet cook had so far been limited to boiling eggs, making peanut butter sandwiches and the like. However the mess sergeant happened to be one of the top mess sergeants in the Air Corps. Naturally our inspections were right out of the top drawer and we got rave reviews.

Shortly after reporting to Galveston I became officer of the day, which meant that for twenty-four hours you are on duty with a saber at your side, representing the commanding officer, no matter what. "What" in my case meant that a fire that broke out on the base and also a prisoner escaped from the guardhouse and took off over the causeway from Galveston to the mainland. This is getting your feet wet in a hurry; but thanks to my failing memory I've forgotten how that night turned out.

The daily routine at the base included practice dive bombing which was done in a swampy piece of Texas outside the aerodrome. Live bombs were released at the end of a dive on ground targets on the ground. This operation was usually fairly peaceful but occasionally we had to go in on the ground and search for duds that hadn't exploded. This was even more exciting than the actual bombing.

I was on the team that represented the group at the national gunnery matches held at Langley Field, Virginia. I came in twelfth in this match that included machine gunnery at ground targets as well as aerial tow targets and dive-and level-bombing. Christie Mathesin, Jr., son of the baseball king, was also in the match. My time for the meet came during the middle of the day when the air currents off the swamp made for very bumpy air throwing me off my best performance. At least that is my alibi for being only twelfth in the nation.

Hometown Springfield was not too far off course on the return to Galveston, and I persuaded the C.O. to allow me to return that way. Again the thrill of all thrills, this was having your own combat plane without the prying eyes of your superior officers on a hometown visit, and I made the most of it. Long before reaching Springfield, I got down on the deck and roared at treetop level through the town past the hospital, lacing the arrival with other dives on other ground objects including my own homestead.

The family was there at the airport to greet me, and I gave my grandmother, father, mother, sister and two brothers each a real airplane ride. For years afterward I was referred to locally as that Recknagel kid who kept the patients awake at the hospital.

Among the officers stationed with us at Galveston was one Captain Idzorick, who had fought with General Pershing against Pancho Villa. His first love was horses; and second, airplanes. Our group had originally been used as observation planes for watching the Mexicans across the border and later transferred to Fort Crockett as the Third Attack Group. Captain "Izzy," as he was called, was in charge of the daily morning exercise sessions we had before we began flying our missions. This bit consisted of riding around in circles and performing close-order drills on a bunch of plugs, huge animals who jolted our kidneys out of place. Horses were never my favorite; they are too high off the ground and go too fast. After a while I began to wonder whether I was a member of the flying corps or of the cavalry.

These were fast-moving days serving with this group commanded by Major Davenport Johnson, another World War I participant. Each morning after the horse exercise a mission was flown sometimes just a crosscountry flight low over the ground with crossover turns in nine-ship formations, hopping over trees and fences, or a gunnery mission, shooting our machine guns at targets on the ground or at a large sock towed behind another plane.

Some of these missions turned out to be pretty spicy, such as having your machine gun fail to stop firing even though you were well past the target. Even towing the target sock for a group of reserve artillery officers on weekend duty had its share of excitement. It seems that for aiming purposes they would sight on the towing plane and make allowances for the distance back to the sock. On more than one occasion I thought I was in real combat when the flak started exploding all around me.

Some fifty years later while on a junket to Las Vegas, my wife and I had dinner with another couple, and during the conversation the man mentioned his earlier service in the Artillery Corps at Galveston. He made mention of their sighting practices and was amused to think what might go through the mind of the towing pilot as he was being fired upon. My reply was, "So, you're the one!"

A flight of six of us flew to Tyler, Texas, to dedicate the new Tyler airport. Lieutenant Tommy Thurlow was our flight leader. Later Tommy became the navigator for Howard Hughes on his record flight around the world. When they returned a ticker-tape parade was held on Michigan Boulevard in Chicago, and I watched Hughes and Tommy go by sitting on the back of a touring car. I waved and said, "Hi, Tom," and we had a short conversation as they rolled along.

It was on this visit to Tyler that I met my first wife-to-be, Elizabeth Spence, daughter of a lumber and hardware store owner, Robert Spence, and his wife, Alma Woldert Spence, who was poet laureate of Texas. Mr. Spence was also a Texas Ranger, although this had nothing to do with my marriage to Miss Spence. With the discovery of this new lady friend I found it necessary to make frequent trips to Tyler on training missions. On one occasion I made my usual dives on the town before returning to the airport. Much to my chagrin, when I landed I found the commanding officer's plane sitting in the hangar. He was also visiting Tyler, which was his home town, and he had watched my performance from the ground. The following Monday morning he passed me in the hall at headquarters and casually mentioned that his relatives in Tyler always told him everything that went on.

Our social life at Ft. Crockett was more than adequate for a bunch of young second lieutenants of the Air Corps. The people of Galveston were most cordial, and parties, beach picnics, dances and other social events were plentiful. On the lighter side Charlie Skannal, Jim Going and I shared a house on the beach, complete with a colored housekeeper and whiskey at five dollars per gallon in our own jug. The whiskey was delivered to the back door and came in a rather raw state; but after several weeks in a charcoal-lined keg in the trunk of my roadster it became a smooth brand of sipping whiskey.

Other amenities at the fort included a duck hunting camp about forty-five minutes flying time south on Matagorda Island, a long stretch of primitive beach blessed by the absence of people and whose only residents were seagulls, jellyfish, ducks, geese, and skunks. The camp itself was a cabin equipped with bunks, a kitchen and an Army cook who fed us well. Hunting the ducks and the geese was done from numerous blinds in the area.

One night at this camp, while sleeping on a cot, I was awakened by a sound somewhat like gritting teeth. There, a few inches from my face, was a civet cat staring at me and making menacing noises. I kept my cool and didn't move a muscle, and he slowly walked away. I am really proud of my poise under such duress. A nest of these critters roomed under the floor of the cabin, and later, when the cook tried to coax them to leave, they complied—but not without leaving their calling card. The cabin became livable some weeks later.

While flying down to one of these hunting safaris I caught up with a flock of geese and followed right along with them at my indicated air speed of ninety miles per hour, so you can say that the geese can cruise along with the best of us—not at Mach 2, but at the leisurely pace of ninety miles per hour.

Many well-known people visited us at the base. Jack

Dempsey, the boxer, popped in and was given a ride in one of our snappiest formations, including crossover turns close to the ground, dive-bombing and other tricks of the trade. As he sat on his parachute the upper part of his body protruded well out into the slipstream. He later made a comment to the press that two things in his life he would never forget: the time he was knocked out of the ring by Firpo, and the hairy ride he had with the Third Attack Group.

A navy training submarine dropped anchor in the Galveston harbor one day with its noncommissioned officer and a number of cadets. Such guests were always given the formation treatment to make them feel welcome. In return, some of our pilots were given a ride in their rusty-looking sub, which was anchored in about fifteen feet of water in the harbor. Once everyone was aboard the noncom shouted the order to dive and one end of the sub and only one end hit the bottom, with everybody and everything sailing to that end. After some heavy-duty Navy-type bellowing by the noncom, the other end fell to the ocean floor with a dull thud. After this indoctrination into the art of submarinery we offered the tars another even more sophisticated formation ride, but they declined. Submarinery was never my favorite branch of the service.

The annual Patrick Trophy race with attack planes was held at Fort Crockett. Nineteen pilots from the fort took part in this, the speed classic of the day. The race was conducted over a ten-mile triangular course, with six laps flown at an altitude of a few feet above the ground. A record speed of 149 miles per hour was set during this event by Tex Westley, and since I took three seconds longer I came in second. My trophy, awarded by the Galveston Chamber of Commerce, was an engraved silver cigarette chest.

One of our major maneuvers was the great Air Corps demonstration of 1931, in which every Army plane that could get into the air participated—some 600 aircraft. The various groups from all over the country landed at several fields near the demonstration area to regroup and form the greatest aerial parade in history. That number of planes in the air was exceeded only by our mass bombing of Europe during World War II, some ten years later. In New York we were feted by the mayor and other notables, after which we put on a big parade down the Hudson and past Battery Park. It must have been quite a sight to the many hundreds of thousands who gathered to watch. I would have liked to see this bash myself, but I was buried right in the middle of the formation and all I could see was wings, wheels, heads and tails. Lindbergh was also one of the participants.

Then it was on to Baltimore for another similar show. Upon landing there I called a high school friend from Springfield, the Reverend Adrian Pheiffer, who had a parish just outside of town. He and his wife invited me out to dinner that evening, and during the conversation Adrian mentioned that some day he would like to take an airplane ride with me—someday, that is. Why not tomorrow, I asked? Come along with us; I can arrange it. He wasn't too sure that this was such a good idea, but his wife chimed in and said this was his big chance, so he agreed to go. The next morning he showed up and a sergeant fitted him with helmet and goggles and instructions on how to use the parachute in case some of us flew too close to each other and had to bail out. Should he land in the Potomac, he was warned, he was to swim quickly away from the silk 'chute so that he would not be suffocated by it. Again he was not too sure about the whole thing, but he threw caution to the wind and didn't chicken out. Later he wrote a comprehensive article in the Springfield *News-Sun* about the Wright Brothers and the progress of aviation, and made reference to this flight and his part in the dedication of the Arlington Bridge. Looking down he had seen President and Mrs. Herbert Hoover watching our aerial parade. I didn't see the president and his wife because I was busy, but many years later I had lunch with Mr. Hoover at the Omaha, Nebraska, airport, and we talked about a few things.

All was not serious stuff on this trip, and occasionally some clowning had to enter the picture. One of our finest gags occurred in Baltimore when we hired a lady of the evening to go

out on a date with our deputy commander. For obvious reasons
it was more enjoyable to pull such stunts on your superiors—
provided, of course, that you didn't get caught. We paid the lady
in advance and swore her to secrecy, and she posed as just a
sweet demure young creature out on a date with a handsome Air
Corps lieutenant. It is quite possible that we will never know if
we got our money's worth, and none of us will ever ask.

After Baltimore we moved on to several other cities where we
performed the same program, including a visit to the waterfront
in Chicago. It was at this point that I turned over the controls to
the crew chief for a brief rest. There followed some gyrations
and erratic dips, so I took over again. On landing I found that
the crew chief had indulged in a few more spirits that were necessary the night before. I have no idea how he got back to Fort
Crockett, but he didn't fly home with me.

Our commandant, Major Johnson, received transfer orders,
and it was a sad day for the group. We were a closely knit bunch
of officers and men, highly trained in attack aviation and good
friends as well, and we hated to have the group broken up.

As the major and his wife prepared to leave his command all
of the officers and men gathered around to wish them both the
best. After the ceremony he appeared to be disappointed that an
aerial review had not been staged in his honor. But unbeknownst
to him, a large white cross had been pointed on the top of his
car, and when he sadly drove away on the road to Houston, all
three squadrons of attack planes, thirty-nine in all, dove on his
car with a mighty roar in a final salute to the "old man." He
must have got a lump in his throat from this final tribute from
his boys.

My own departure at the termination of my active duty was
somewhat subdued by comparison, but the lump in my throat
was the same. I packed my worldly goods in the Model A Ford
roadster, shook hands with a few friends, and headed for my
hometown of Springfield, out of a job and facing a full-blown
depression.

Third Attack Group, 1930–1932.
Opposite above: Major Davenport Johnson, commander.
Opposite below: Officers of the unit.
Above: Base aerodrome, a small dirt sandy stretch of beach.
Below: The Curtiss Falcon A-3, workhorse of the group.
(Photos: 1st Photo Section, Air Corps, U.S. Army,
Ft. Sam Houston, Texas.)

90th Attack Squadron, 1930–1932.
Opposite, above: Officers and crewmen.
Opposite, below: Flying officers ready for takeoff.
Above: Flight officers.
Bottom row (l–r): Lt. John Snadow; Lt. Oscar Beal;
Lt. Dan Jenkins; Capt. Virgil Hines, commander;
Lt. Tex Westley; Lt. Fred Talley.
Top row (l–r): Lt. Ford Fair; Lt. Clayton Stiles;
Lt. Ted Landon, who led a flight of B-17s approaching Hawaii
when Pearl Harbor was attacked;
Lt. Frank Stewart; Lt. Carl Recknagel; Lt. Bob Easton
(Photos: U.S. Army Air Corps.)

50 ■

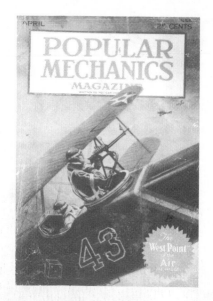

Above: Popular Mechanics *cover, April 1930.*
(Copyright, the Hearst Corporation, all rights reserved).
Below: No. 43, flown by the author in the
Patrick Trophy race, 1930.

*Above: Attack planes taking off for the Patrick Trophy race.
Below: Rounding a pylon during the race. No. 43 is the lower
plane. The upper plane cut the pylon and was disqualified.
(Photos: U.S. Army Air Corps, Ft. Sam Houston, Texas.)*

NINETEEN PLANES WILL ENTER SENSATIONAL TROPHY TRIALS; VISITING SHIPS ARE COMING

Thousands Expected to View Thrilling Events; Formation Flying, Parachute Jumps All on Program; High Officials of Service Will Be at Flying Field

The most thrilling and spectacular aviation event ever to be held here will be staged this afternoon, when 19 pilots of the Third Attack Group take their places at the start of the Mason M. Patrick trophy race, an aerial event open only to members of the attack group now stationed at Galveston.

Undaunted by a recent crash which took the life of their comrade, the pilots, led by Maj. Davenport Johnson, their commanding officer, will compete for the Patrick trophy, with thousands of visitors from all sections of the state, high ranking army officials and numerous aviation enthusiasts expected to swell the crowd of Galvestonians which will be present.

Parachute Jumps.

Prior to the spectacular speed classic, 24 army ships from San Antonio will give demonstrations participated in by observation, bombing and pursuit planes.

As a climax to the race, parachute jumps will be executed by Corpl. Joe Collier and Pvt. Bruce Karns from a Ford transport plane, 2,500 feet in the air.

Yesterday the last motor of the A3B attack planes was checked over and the speed tests completed. Today the planes, when they go out over the Gulf of Mexico in formation will go aloft complete except for vital parts of their machine guns and with empty bomb racks.

The race is to be of 60 miles length, six times around a triangular course marked by aviation pylons, two of which are on west beach and one near the Bay Shore Golf Club.

Selection of pilots was made last Sunday and the flyers immediately started elimination tryouts on Monday, when Lt. A. N. Booth of the Eighth Squadron was injured fatally in a crash.

Five of the pilots were drawn by lot from each of the tactical squadrons, the Eighth, 13th and 90th squadrons, and three from the 60th Service Squadron. Maj. Johnson making the 19th entry. One man will accompany each of the pilots as crew chief.

The assignment of places was made tentatively in the following order: Maj. D. Johnson, Second Lt. C. E. Recknagel, Second Lt. L. C. Westley, Second Lt. R. K Taylor, Second Lt C. Stiles, Second Lt. J. B. Bell, Second Lt. J. B. Nedwed, Second Lt. M. M. Beach, Second Lt. R. L. Easton, Second Lt J. A. Anderson, Second Lt. W. H. Sykes, First Lt. R. F. Stearley, Second Lt J. C. Neely, Second Lt. R. J. Gibbons, Second Lt. J. H.

(See TROPHY RACE, Page 12.)

Race Program

National interest is centering on the sensational Gen. Mason M. Patrick trophy race this afternoon. The program follows:

1:30 P. M.—Bombers clear airdrome.

1:35 P. M.—Observation planes clear airdrome.

1:45 P. M.— Pursuit planes clear airdrome.

1:55 P.M.—Third Attack Group (27 planes) clear airdrome.

2 to 2:10 P. M.—First event—observation formation.

2:10 to 2:50 P. M.—Second event—bombers in formation.

2:25 to 2:30 P. M.—Third event—pursuit formation.

2:35 to 2:45 P. M.—Pursuit acrobatics—three planes.

2:45 to 3:05 P. M.—Attack Group formation—27 planes.

3:10 P. M.—Bombers land and taxi to assigned position.

3:13 P. M.—BT's land and taxi to assigned position.

3:20 P.M.—Pursuit planes land and taxi to assigned position.

3:25 P. M.—Attack planes not in race land and taxi to assigned position.

3:30 P.M.—Attack race starts.

Racing planes form in squadron and land after race.

Parachute jump immediately after racing planes land.

CHAPTER 4

The Depression

ARRIVING IN SPRINGFIELD I started looking for a job of which there were precious few. One came my way as an airport manager and chief pilot of the Johnson Flying service at the Dayton airport. The job consisted of running the airport, testing flares for the International Flare Signal Company of Tippicanoe City, special crosscountry flights, local passenger hops, weekly air shows, servicing transient aircraft, and any other excuse to get an airplane into the air or glean a buck in some way.

The flight equipment consisted of a Curtiss Pusher, an Aeronca, a Wright J-5 Waco, a J-5 Travelair, an OX-powered Swallow and a Kinner Bird, a real collection of the oldies, any one of which would be worthy of a spot in the Smithsonian today.

The weekly air shows were noteworthy. Entertainment was the name of the game, whether it was entertainment for the spectators or for the performers. We had a parachute jumper who jumped at night with twirling colored flashlights. His words on leaving the wing were "see you in a few minutes." He was a real stunt man and did many shows for us. In one jump his main 'chute split in two and he had to use his backpack emergency 'chute. The 'chute that failed was the one I always used when I did my aerial didoes, but I never wore a backup.

About a year later I met him again and he was completely crippled. He had tried a new stunt by diving from a fifty-foot tower into a large wooden tub of water, when the tub disintegrated. It seems ironic to get hurt in this fashion after all of the aerial stuff he had been through, but of course astronaut John Glenn slipped in his bathtub and got a concussion.

There was no end to our innovations. We raced a plane against a motorcycle, bursted balloons with our propellers, bombed targets with flour bags, had dead-stick landing contests, and of course stunting all over the sky. One exhibit which worked well was dropping a duck fitted with a small silk parachute from 1000 feet up. This guy was proud of his work and made many drops. He would squawk all the way down, landing gracefully and walking around proudly trailing his 'chute. He did this act for weeks, a real ham. We kept him behind the hangar, but one night a weasel got into his pen and his career was over. His place in the world was alongside the parachute jumper and other greats.

Between times back in Dayton I set a possible record in the Aeronca. Starting at one mile up the engine was shut down and I did fifteen dead-stick loops, the last one ending with the landing. I also tried a spin from a mile up but had to call it off when the wing showed signs of buckling. Another record was set by one of our lady students. Mrs. Iona Coppedge, who weighed in at only ninety-five pounds. She climbed the Aeronca to 14,000 feet, probably because the plane was nearly empty.

The flying service at one point owed me a little money in back wages which showed little promise of being paid off. I wrangled a deal with Al Johnson whereby I would fly down to Tyler, Texas, to get married to Peggy Spence, the girl I had courted while at Fort Crockett. An airplane on one's honeymoon was pure luxury in those times.

This being my first experience with marriage, I had a lot of learning ahead. The new wife brought her luggage to the airport, and by baggage I mean one suitcase after another. No thought was given to weight control for the little plane and on takeoff we rolled and rolled until I finally grunted over the fence and made it into the air. One of the overloading factors was the thirty pairs of shoes along with the bags. Brides come with a lot of baggage and as I found out later, girls in general always travel with plenty of the heavy stuff.

New friend Ralph Lee gave my new bride and myself one side

of a duplex he owned in Dayton. The other side was occupied by a nice Jewish lady, Mrs. Litwitz. She immediately took over my new bride and coached her in the facts of life, including how to deal with humans of the opposite sex and how to put up with their weird, ugly habits. She was a very dear friend and had a very important effect later in our lives.

Friend Ralph Lee swung a nice flying job my way, since he was in a position to do so as head of General Motors' public relations. The assignment was to fly a Buhl Air Sedan with a movie camera aboard photographing test runs of new autos rolling around the proving grounds. This movie was to be used at the General Motors exhibit at the Chicago World Fair of 1933. Sally Rand also made her contribution.

On arriving at the Detroit airport I contacted the owner of the Buhl to start the assignment. He pointed to the flying machine and said there it is. I questioned him about my qualifications to fly this bird, since it was the first time I had ever seen one and did he want to check me out? He replied, "That's a good idea. You can take it around the field and I'll watch you." Now that's what I call a checkout.

One day at the Dayton airport we were selling rides when a young couple approached me and started asking questions about how safe it was to fly, and so forth. I did my best selling job on this pair, explaining the mechanics of an airplane as well as offering my vast flying experience as an extra safety factor. They finally agreed to take a ride with me, one at a time, in the little Aeronca.

The next morning a fighter plane from Wright Field zoomed over the field and slow-rolled along the road into Dayton until out of sight. The pilot of the plane came back later and to my embarrassment tuned out to be the same man I'd sold a bill of goods the day before and conned him into taking an airplane ride. He was Lieutenant Irv Woodring of the original Three Musketeers, the other two being Charles Lindbergh and George Price. Eventually I got over my chagrin and we became friends. One evening we invited him and his wife over for dinner when I got the word that a new fighter plane being tested by Woodring had just disintegrated and spread over a city block.

OUR boss at Dayton was Al Johnson, who had pilot's license number three—numbers one and two being held by Orville and Wilbur Wright, of course. My earnings were not much, sometimes as little as seventy-five dollars a month, but during the Depression that was a comfortable sum. Anyone who has not experienced the Great Depression cannot realize the depths of despair some families experienced. And of course anyone who could afford the price of flying instruction was nothing less than a bloated plutocrat. A few determined students had to cut short on their food money to eke out a few minutes of aerial instruction.

We offered a bargain instruction package for seventy-five dollars, which included a complete course in ground school and flight training up to one solo flight. Two of our class members, the Halls, were identical twins of the affluent class. They looked exactly alike, even down to the small space between their upper teeth, drove identical yellow roadsters and clowned all over the place. I once saw one of them scratch his initials on the other's car in fun. But their best caper was the flying course which they purchased at the price of seventy-five dollars for one person. Each twin would show up for instruction on different days until finally one of them soloed after an unusually long period of instruction. Then the next day the other twin rented the plane and did his solo. I knew about this scam but went along with it since good customers were hard to come by in those days.

ONE of our aircraft was the Aeronca, dubbed the "flying bath tub." This little two-cylinder number was designed by Jean Roche who was the chief civilian engineer at Wright Field. I taught him to fly in his own designed airplane. Between us we decided to enter this little gem in the American Air Races of 1933, to be held at Midway Field in Chicago. To further our chances in the race, Mr. Roche had the landing gear removed and replaced by a single wheel and two small wheels on the wing tips. Upon landing this new plane would gradually tip over until it rode on one of the wingtip wheels; for takeoffs it required a person on the ground to steady the wings until adequate air speed was reached. On the trip to Chicago landings were made for refueling at several airports along the way. The folks I borrowed for the takeoffs must still be talking about this weird flying machine.

On one of the stops I arranged to visit Lieutenant Ralph Sterling, a friend from Fort Crockett days. He operated a gaggle of slot machines in a small town west of Indianapolis. He invited me into a back room where these machines were calibrated to ensure that their owners received a fair amount of profit for their investment.

The American Air races were to be flown over a triangular course, and my early training with the Third Attack Group told me that the downwind legs were to be flown well off the ground in order to take advantage of the wind, while the upwind legs should be flown hugging the ground.

In the first race I finished third among the other specially designed racing craft, but I bowed out of the second race when I heard several of the other pilots discussing how they were going to "get" that silly Aeronca. I took my prize money of $150 and left for home. Those racing pilots had been preparing their craft for this event for a year, and they weren't about to let some hayseed pilot with a flying bathtub take any more of their prize money.

> *A tail wind is a misty hope*
> *Wrought in every pilot's mind*
> *That once in all the years*
> *Will blow from behind*
> *Will blow from where he thinks he is*
> *To where he hopes he goes*
> *Yet every pilot knows there are no winds*
> *Save those upon the nose.*

Some fifty years later, on an Easter visit to Springfield, we visited the toy house of Jonathan Winters, which was located in back of a funeral home where services were held for my grandmother, mother, and father. We saw an old grade-school classmate of mine by the name of Clarence Metz, and my brother asked him, "Do you remember Carl?" Clarence took a look at me and decided he had never heard of me. But all of a sudden he said, "Oh, now I remember you. You're the guy who scared the hell out me at the Dayton airport!" It's nice to be remembered for something, whatever it may be.

While visiting the Cleveland air races some time later I ran into Maurice Wiley, who had just gotten a job as copilot with United Airlines at the fabulous rate of $200 per month, which topped my earnings at the flying service considerably, and he recommended I apply, too. I drove to Chicago for the job and was interviewed by Bert Lott. He knew Al Johnson and asked if I would mind if he gave Al a call. His feet were on the desk and as he talked to Al he frowned from time, laughed and shook his head. I don't know what went on in this conversation, but I got the job and was on my way to an airline career that lasted thirty-three years, until my retirement in 1966.

The Johnson Flying Services, Dayton, Ohio, 1932.
Above: "The fleet."
Below (l–r): Jean Roche, civilian engineer at McKook and
Wright Field; Carl Recknagel, chief pilot;
Iona Coppedge, student; Al Johnson, owner.

American Air Races, 1933.
Above: The one-wheel Aeronca C-3 with wheel coweled in.
Below: The One-wheel Aeronca leading the parade of racers to start the race.

Above: Waco biplane. Phil Herzing (left), owner of the
St. Mary's Woolen Mills; Carl Recknagel (right).
Below: Ralph Lee and his Kinner Bird.

CHAPTER 5
Up the Ladder

SO AGAIN WE GATHERED our meager belongings, rented a trailer and made off for Chicago for the new job with the magnificent salary. My commercial career was launched. On the way to Chicago, while going down a slight grade, I looked over and saw the trailer pass me and end up in a ditch. Apparently it had broken loose, and without the braking effect of an engine it had decided to outrun me.

At UAL headquarters in Chicago I was assigned to the eastern division, which extended from Chicago to Newark, the eastern terminus of the transcontinental route. The duties of a copilot—or mate, as we were called then—were to make sure the captain's bag was aboard, refuel the airplane en route and, on flights dispatched without a stewardess, to serve the gourmet meals, which consisted of a cold chicken leg and some potato salad stuffed in a box plus a little lukewarm coffee from a thermos jug.

For a passenger to be served such an attractive meal by the hairy arm of a copilot who had just refueled the plane at the previous stop was not the wave of the future in air travel. But by the time I arrived on the scene some of these undesirable arrangements had been phased out. A certain Steve Simpson had promoted the idea of having nurses serve as cabin attendants. This would help the passenger overcome his fear of flying and would offer a nicer way of serving food and beverages than the earlier greasy, hairy arm method. It was a giant step forward and became an instant success, since no man, however frightened by flying, would ever show his apprehension to a charming lass. Why do dentists have attractive ladies minding the dental chair? I too have the same tendency, like one day while eating a roast

63

beef sandwich in a restaurant in Manhattan Beach a waiter across the counter was slicing some more beef and sliced off his thumb, which fell on the slicing board. He raved and ranted and seemed more upset about his thumb than about any pain he might have been having. I stared at his isolated thumb and tried to finish my sandwich just to show off my macho nature to the waitress, but a few minutes later I pushed my plate aside and left the restaurant, never to return.

THERE were numerous happenings in the eastern division, and there were few flights that didn't bring out something of interest. On one westbound flight from Newark to Cleveland we had a very strong headwind, which called for flying low over the ground. The captain on this trip was the same Charlie Thompson who had escorted us new arrivals from the train at March Field in Riverside four years earlier. Thompson had instructed me never to touch a thing unless he told me to, so when one gas tank ran dry I did nothing, and both engines of the Boeing 247 quit. Thompson came on the overhead intercom yelling, "Change the tanks, you dumb dodo!" while he looked around for a place to set the plane down if the engines didn't respond. But I had followed his instructions to the letter, so why should he be so upset?

In those days irregular operations were the rule, not the exception. Weather was the main culprit. About midway between Cleveland and Newark we had an emergency landing strip carved out of the wooded wild country up in the hills of Pennsylvania. This strip was used many times to wait for improvement in the weather at our destination. Here the sleeping quarters for both passengers and crew were in the airplane that was brought in. One night in the dark I stepped on a bundle of blankets on the floor of the plane and the voice of Harry Richmond, the movie and radio singer, bellowed out one of his loudest oratorios. I apologized but he only grunted, "Don't worry about it."

The forest around this dirt strop abounded in deer, bear, and other wildlife. Deer were a nuisance, especially at night, and we often had to chase them off with our landing lights before we could take off. I recall one night when I reported by radio to Cleveland "delay on account of deer on field," and some wit came on the air and asked if she was attractive.

Flying the line was down to earth—figuratively and literally. It actually amounted to barnstorming on a schedule. Each pilot created his own brand of navigation, with such aids as landmarks, a line of beacons, a few crude radio aids, or even asking the copilot where he thought they were. On the ground we had dispatchers who fed us weather reports and anything else that might be of interest. On some dismal nights the dispatcher assisted by telling the pilot, "I can hear you...you're passing over the field right now." But our own special aids were essential when static interrupted the deal. In the end, all decisions of any importance came right out of the cockpit however.

On another snowy evening I was flying as copilot with Johnny Ames when we noticed a hatch not securely fastened and flapping in the breeze. We landed at La Porte, Indiana, and I got out and tried to climb up the wing which was slippery with snow, and after several sliding attempts were made I made it up to the flapping hatch. The hatch was fastened and we took off and no one was ever the wiser. This made us a few minutes late at Cleveland but was airline flying at its best for the times. Johnny later became a justice of the peace in Northern California.

About that time something called air traffic control began as a gleam in someone's eye. Until then, traffic control meant avoiding collisions with other aircraft; if you saw someone coming your way, you made an effort to dodge him. But all such precautions are useless if you're in the soup and can't see a thing. Nevertheless, we invented our own traffic control techniques. For example, one stormy night around Cleveland, when the stuff was thick and heavy, the skipper of another airline was having some difficulty pinpointing his exact position, which he knew to be somewhere in Ohio, probably near Cleveland. I was copilot for Captain Harold Knoop, and we were also in the Cleveland area, and Knoop realized that some form of traffic control was needed. So he called the other pilot and asked which quadrant of the four-legged radio range he was in. The other pilot quickly reported he was in quadrant A, and Harold told him sternly, "Now you stay in A and I'll stay in N." This early form of traffic control may seem crude by present standards, but it was effective in its day.

My own encounter with traffic lights of the air came while flying from Newark to Cleveland with Charlie Peoples, a real old-timer. Newark called us and said that Air Traffic Control had cleared us to fly to Cleveland at 6000 feet. Charlie looked at me and asked "What was that?" I admitted that I didn't know, so he picked up his mike and said, "You tell ATC to go to hell!" This may have been the first and last clearance ever issued by this controller.

Living conditions on the road were not too comfortable in those days, but if one is really bushed, almost anything will do. Most of the layovers were spent in places called "dog houses," mostly cold hangars with the barest of comforts. One exception was the eastern layover at the Newark Athletic Club, where we enjoyed all the privileges of club members. But the rooms were occupied by six or more of us at a time, and although the beds were comfortable we all had different departure and arrival times, so all night long the telephone would ring with a wakeup call for someone to go to work, or someone else would come stumbling in from a trip.

Charlie Blair was one of the copilots doing this act, but he had other plans in mind for his future. He would extend his trips beyond Chicago to Salt Lake City just to build up his fortitude by flying from Salt Lake back to Newark. He also married Maureen O'Hara, the green-eyed movie actress, and became a general in the Air Force during World War II. After the war he started his own airline in the Caribbean, but a fatal mishap ended his career.

The Chicago doghouse fit the usual pattern—a room or two in one corner of a cold hangar equipped with double-decked bunk beds and a basic toilet. On one of my three-day layovers I occupied the upper deck. I left my heavy woolen socks on for warmth, and when I had occasion to crawl down to visit the restroom I stepped right into the mouth of the sleeper below me, stuffing the well-used sock into his mouth and eliciting a gagging sound somewhat like a chain saw hitting a nail in a tree. I had no regrets, though, for he had been doing his thing all night long.

The Cleveland doghouse was a jewel among the many. It was a shack next to the hangar, and during the winter months this Mecca was the survival of the fittest. There was nothing quiet about the place day or night. Crew members came and went at all hours; the one toilet operated some of the time; and airplanes were revving up just outside the hangar. Sleeping there was an art form. During the winters snow often drifted in through the leaky windows, covering our cots, and the blankets were rationed. Sometimes a loud scream could be heard in the middle of the night: "Who stole my blanket?"

Later, however, our layovers moved up to top-drawer accommodations such as the Plaza Hotel (where rates are now $340 per night and up) and the Saint Moritz, both on Central Park in New York City. A one-day stopover in the big city was always interesting, and just roaming around the streets one could see the rich and famous strolling along. Movie stars and extras as well as politicians and sports luminaries were among the strollers. Good old Jack Dempsey could often be seen strolling by with a young chickadee on each arm or sitting in his restaurant nearby. The doorman at the St. Moritz was a friendly fellow, especially to us flyers. While waiting for our limo to arrive he would point out many of the characters staying at the hotel. He pointed out a Cadillac with a chauffeur pulling up and discharging a pompously dressed guy and told me that the man was a four-flusher who rented the Caddy from month to month and always put on a show worthy of a modern magnate. He also pointed out ladies of the evening making their rounds, and even indicated the recipients of their favors. My favorite comment of his was, "You airline pilots are the real people."

One night on the so-called "hell stretch" between Chicago

and Newark most of the terminals had been closed by fog, and our trip in a Boeing 247 had to make a run for it to the only place fit for landing—Toledo, Ohio. Our one and only passenger was Wallace Beery, of movie fame, who had made many trips with us before.

Also on the flight were two bags of U.S. Post Office registered mail, which I as copilot was tagged with the responsibility of delivering to the Chicago post office by rail. Wearing my shoulder gun and with my two mail pouches under lock and key, Wallace Beery and I made our way into the Toledo terminal to join up with the train to Chicago. When we arrived at the terminal we walked up to a small orange juice stand and he ordered a glass of juice. The little girl behind the counter was overwhelmed when she saw this famous movie star in person, but we got our juice. This was in the early thirties, when movie stars were something not of this world.

We boarded the train to Chicago and I slept on my two bags of registered mail with my gun at the ready. But when we arrived at Gary, Indiana, two United Airlines cargo men climbed in and quickly made off with my two charges. So I blew it. But it turned out okay, because they were sent there to pick up the pouches and deliver them to the Chicago post office.

On another westbound flight from Newark, the Cleveland weather was down and out, so my captain, Slim Larned, set her down at the Kylertown emergency field to wait for an improvement in the Cleveland weather. Our crew—Slim, myself and one stewardess—repaired to a small hotel in nearby Phillipsburg. Now it would have been easy to get your rest here except that every hour on the hour all night long the field called in to report that the weather in Cleveland hadn't changed a bit. This wasn't a night for rest and sleep. In addition to the frequent telephone calls, suddenly there was a commotion outside our window. Looking out we saw towering flames when a lumber yard next door had caught fire. The stewardess in her nightie joined us to watch this spectacle in the snowy night. Four men hauled up a water pumper on wheels to fight the blaze. Eventually we returned to our cots for another try at sleeping.

The next morning during the taxi ride out to the field, Slim mentioned to me that he had dreamed that he heard another United pilot in the area, Captain Clarence Hudson, calling Kylertown asking them to try to find out which town he was circling in the snow storm. This was par for the course in those days except that I had also had the same dream.

At that point the taxi driver assured us that it had been no dream. It seems he was a ham radio buff and had heard Hudson's request for information and had called the field to relay the information that Hudson was over Phillipsburg. This radio man and taxi driver lived in the hotel room next to ours, and instead of dreaming this fantastic drama we were actually hearing the entire episode.

None of these spicy events of the 1930s could happen today, but even better ones must be in the making. Somewhat before my time, a dispatcher at Cheyenne called a Captain Frank Crissman for a report on his position. Crissman replied that he was seventy-three miles east of Rock Springs, Wyoming. "How do you verify seventy-three miles?" asked the dispatcher. Frank came back with "On account of a snow squall I've landed on the Lincoln Highway. A sign here says 'Rock Springs—73 miles.' As soon as the squall passes I'll take off."

Another time, on an icy night over the Rockies between Salt Lake and Cheyenne, the following conversation between two 40-B mail pilots was heard:

[First pilot]: "I'm picking up a lot of ice....The air speed is falling off fast."

[Second]: "Keep in touch, old boy."

[First]: "It's down to 80 [miles per hour]. Now it's 70 ...60...[long pause]...Well, it must have just been the airspeed indicator!"

Other intimate cockpit quotes I recall from this era are:

[Captain to copilot]: "You too can become senior."

"The signal began to fade, so I knew I was past the station."

"Hold this thing in a bank while I try to pry open my iced-up window so I can see to land."

"Can you see anything out your side? I can't see a damn thing over here."

[Flight engineer to captain]: "Sir, the runway is over there."

IN the early days of aerial wireless transmissions it was standard practice to radio ahead the names of the crew members aboard a plane. But for some reason my name, Recknagel, was a tough one to digest. The messages were relayed from Newark to Kylertown and then on to Cleveland, and sometimes they went awry. One day Red Henry, the dispatcher at Kylertown, was trying to relay the names of my crew, but couldn't quite get the name of the mate. After several attempts he finally gave up and said, "It's no use, Newark, I can't get it. It sounds just like Recknagel to me."

Red wasn't the only one who had trouble with my name. One of the great stewardesses, Mary O'Conner, had one shortcoming: she always confused me with another pilot by the name of Randecker. I was always Randecker and he was known as Recknagel. We tried repeatedly to correct her, but to no avail. About twenty years later I ran into Mary in Los Angeles, and she greeted me with, "Hello, Randecker! Do you remember when I used to get you confused with Recknagel?"

One foggy night on an eastbound trip, Captain "Pop" Sterling and I attempted to land at the Kylertown strip to refuel and wait for the weather on the eastern seaboard to improve. We made several attempts to find the ground, but we only got an occasional glimpse of a misty tree-top in the darkness, not enough to accomplish a landing. We gave up on Kylertown and headed east to Sunbury, Pennsylvania, where we knew there was a landing strip with a green beacon on an island in the Susquehana River. The strip was located and we set down to await better weather over the east and to replenish our dry gas tanks, glad that we didn't have any passengers aboard to worry about. The captain, the stewardess and I wrapped ourselves in blankets and tried to sleep until morning, when we would call for a gas truck to come out from the mainland so we could continue on to Newark.

"HELLZAPOPPIN" was one of the zaniest Broadway stage shows of that time, and was staged by Ole Olson and Johnson. Ole was a frequent passenger on many of our United flights, and on one he invited Captain Dusty Rhoades and myself to attend his show. We went to the show, and it was something else. An audience winner of a twenty-five-pound block of ice got it on his lap. Another winner had a cackling rooster placed on his lap.

After the performance Dusty and I crossed the stage behind the curtain to recover our overcoats just as the curtain opened and in full view of the audience two confused airline pilots stood there in the center of the stage with a stupid look on our faces. Ole later thought that this was one of his most hilarious scenes.

Many years later Dusty became General Douglas MacArthur's personal pilot in the Pacific conflict of World War II and has written a great book about his adventures with the general.

Flights during this period of time required progress reports, which consisted mostly of geographic spots by such means as visually sighting something on the ground, enterprising interpretation of the situation, a portion of guesswork laced with some surmise or even asking the copilot where he thought you were.

As often as not, the reporting points were selected on the basis of their wit or innuendo. For example, some of these gems might be "Just south of Middlesex," "Over Blue Ball," "Opposite Three-Fingered Jack," "Next to the Three Sisters," "Passing Molly's Nipple," "Passing Molly's Other Nipple," "Nellie crossing the Delaware," and others. But the landmark I liked best was the radio tower of station WIND, south of Chicago Midway. Every United pilot approaching Midway airport from the east felt compelled to report his position as "passing WIND."

One tower operator at Midway apparently got fed up with this United cornball reporting and was waiting for the time and place. And so it happened, our man reported passing WIND, whereupon the tower operator answered, "I don't care about your physical condition—just give me your position!"

In the mid-30s thunderstorms and tornadoes were always on the menu. Trying to avoid them was fun, but getting caught in one was another matter. While I was flying as copilot with Captain Bob Ashley, a veteran of World War I who later flew with the now-defunct Pan American, we ran into a widespread dust storm over Nebraska, with the visibility down to nothing. Suddenly we hit a shaft of hail, and our DC-3 was riddled from stem to stern. Bob's windshield was smashed, and long tears in the elevator and ailerons made the controls feel like rubber bands. The rocker arms on both engines were bent in, and why they kept running is a big mystery. We limped into Denver, and since my windshield was intact, I made the landing. That gooney bird was one stalwart machine, even though it wouldn't shape up to modern specifications for airline aircraft. This same hail storm destroyed a farm house below us in Akron, Colorado.

The Boeing 247 was gradually eased out by the newer Douglas DC-3, some specimens of which are still flying today, some six decades later. They were the pathfinders of the Normandy invasion during World War II, and were led by Joel Crouch on duty from United. Joel was a fellow steelhead fisherman, and we had some great trips in quest of the gamy ones.

TWA acquired the DC-3 before we at United did and made the most of their speedier airplanes (ten miles per hour faster). Their standard operating procedure out of Midway was to climb for altitude after takeoff and wait for our B-247 to depart, after which they would dive past our plane, thereby showing the passengers of both planes their superior speed. This was frustrating to our pilots, especially since it was routine. However on one flight, my captain, Leo Allen, told me to watch for our friend and let him know when he was about to pass us, which I did. At that point Leo started a steep climb, and the TWA pilot did the same, and as far as I know he is still climbing. Leo then leveled off and resumed cruising speed, easily passing up the TWA speedster on his climb to wherever. Naturally we pointed this out to our passengers with relish.

This fine job with United didn't last too long, however. President Roosevelt canceled the air mail contracts and ordered the Army Air Corps to fly the mail. The equipment and experience of the Army pilots was totally inadequate for this type of flying, and many lives were lost during this fiasco. I saw two of the mishaps in the making, one taking off from Kylertown only to crash in a storm shortly after, the other circling in a snow storm near Goshen, Indiana, the pilot trying to get his bearings and later going in near Toledo.

The cancellation of the air mail contracts forced United to cut back on their personnel, and twenty-five of us new hires were furloughed. By that time I had my new daughter, Margaret Ann, who had arrived by caesarean section at the Chicago Lying In Hospital. Another arrival at the same time was the atomic bomb, which was being developed underneath the tennis courts near the hospital.

So once again we gathered up our meager worldly goods, stowed them in the 1933 Ford roadster and retraced our steps back to Dayton, the cradle of aviation, only this time with another mouth to feed.

A small walk-up flat in Dayton gave us shelter while I looked for some kind of employment, the likes of which were in short supply. My first try was at the Frigidaire assembly plant in Morrain City, just south of Dayton. The waiting room must have had at least fifty or sixty hopefuls gathered in the hiring hall. In the center of the room was a glass enclosed office where the hiring was done. The situation looked pretty grim at this point, but one of the men was staring at me through the glass window. He came out and asked, "Aren't you a friend of Mrs. Litwitz? I think I've seen you over at her place." I got the job, and it was most welcome in these depressed days. Because of zero seniority, this new job was the lowest menial one in the business. I was now a millwright, one who did many greasy jobs around the mile-long assembly line, moving machinery and installing new lines. We became as greasy and oily as one can get, but it was food money. One day while I was working on an especially dirty job, a group of camera men came by on a photo mission, saw me and asked if I was the pilot who had flown them while they were making a movie for General Motors to be shown at the Chicago World's Fair, and what I was doing there. The explanation was simple.

A few weeks later my boss called me in and said that I could no longer have this job. He had just received a letter from the president of General Motors saying that a certain Carl Recknagel was working on a job far below his capabilities and potential and that he should be promoted to something more suitable for his qualifications. I was then moved up to an assignment as a process specification engineer and gladly threw my greasy overalls into the garbage can. *Shades of Ralph Lee and Mrs. Litwitz.*

A RECALL from United Airlines in 1934 brought me and my family back to Chicago to serve for the rest of my career as an airline pilot, except for four years helping Uncle Sam with his problems in World War II.

As with any move, the first order of business is to find shelter for the family. We located a small bungalow in La Grange Park, an easy drive from my workplace at Midway Airport. The day after we moved in, a neighbor lady knocked on the door and asked if she could come in. Recalling our previous experience with our great neighbor lady Mrs. Litwitz, we welcomed her with open arms. Her first question was "Do you young people think that you can afford this place?" The rent was seventy-five dollars per month, which I thought was reasonable enough considering my newly elevated salary of two hundred dollars per month. Now we were finding that there are neighbors and there are neighbors.

Next came a call from the local police chief saying that the trouble-making bitch next door to me had been complaining that "you are driving over the curb to park your car on a paved driveway that was to be used for a future garage on your place."

He said that if I could borrow a sledge hammer and knock the hell out of the curb, everything would be legal. Then he asked me the name of my landlord. Shortly thereafter he called back and told me that the landlord had informed him that I was the best tenant he had ever had, and that I could do anything with the property I wished. So I visited the United stockroom, borrowed a sledge hammer, knocked the hell out of the curb and became legal.

Those early copilot days had their share of happenings, none of which seemed to disturb me in the least. If the captain got himself into a short fuel situation with the weather bad all around and very few places to run to, that was his problem. All I had to do was make sure his bag was aboard, refuel the aircraft, show up on time and keep my yap shut except when I was asked to do otherwise. I could doze through a dazzling thunderstorm, watch the chief maneuver his way around the scud just off the ground and respect him for it. I always felt that if I were called upon, I could do the same.

Then came the switch from the right side of the plane to the left to be in charge of things. Now things would change dramatically. A bolt of lightning across the bow would make me sit up and take notice. Those easy approaches to a foggy landing watched by me had seemed to be a breeze; but now my shoulders had taken on a heavier load.

But the time finally came to check out and get my SATR, or Scheduled Airline Transport Rating, which qualifies one as a captain. Numerous checks under the hood of a biplane called the Boeing 40-B, a former mail plane no longer used as such, were designed to prove one's proficiency. This antique was poorly maintained and not considered worthy of any grooming by the mechanics, since it was out to pasture and was only around to satisfy the whims of a couple of junior types who thought they could become captains. And as for appearances, it was the original shaggy dog.

After a lot of training under the hood, our junior types were pronounced ready to take the big test for their rating. My time came, and the grousy Boeing 40-B was parked at the Midway passenger terminal while I waited for the CAA inspector to show up. He showed up, but took one look at our baby and thought of a dozen reasons why he wanted no part of that flying machine. He hemmed and hawed, but finally agreed to take a chance.

We took off with me in my little hooded cubbyhole in the forward cockpit and the inspector in the back seat. With a fifty-mile-per-hour wind blowing at the time, my test was complicated when it came to the orientation part, where you found yourself lost while approaching a station. The prescribed procedure with this strong wind didn't work out, but I oriented myself and got back over the station, after which we proceeded east over the city of Chicago at a fairly low altitude. Over the heart of the city one fuel tank ran dry and the motor quit. On this plane the gas tank selector happened to be in the rear seat, exactly where the inspector was sitting. I yelled at him above the noise of a quiet engine and told him to reach down and turn the selector valve to another tank. He yelled back and asked "Where is it?" It worked out: he found the selector and changed tanks, and we didn't land in the city of Chicago. I'm sure this inspector didn't want any more of this stuff, so he granted me my SATR and I am now a captain.

CHAPTER 6

United Air Lines

MY FIRST FLIGHT AS A CAPTAIN was from Newark to Cleveland in a Boeing ten-passenger 247 with a full load of passengers and a bad weather condition in Cleveland. Dispatch wanted to short me on fuel because of the load, but we finally made a deal and my crew and I went into the plane to start the trip. At the terminal there were two airliners parked for loading, one of them an American Airlines DC-3, the other our B-247 just behind. When my copilot, Lowell Heacock, and I entered the cockpit I noticed a thin layer of early-morning frost on top of the wings. I'm not a soothsayer or any of those things, but this frost bugged me—call it a hunch or whatever. Seated in the cockpit, I told Lowell, "Let's see how American does when they take off." This was a masterful decision, or maybe just a lucky one, but we watched the American plane leave the gate and try to lift off several times with no success, finally going through the dike at the end of the runway and spinning like a top in the swamp.

By this time I started to leave the cockpit to have the mechanics tow our aircraft into the hangar to melt off the ice on the wings, after which we completed the trip without incident. Lady luck entered the picture here, but we established the fact that any interference on the upper surface of the wings affects the lift, since about two thirds of the lift comes from the upper wing surface.

Yet some five decades later an airliner taking off from Washington National Airport during a melting snow condition crashed into the bridge across the Potomac because of ice on the upper surface of the wings. Still another, more recent attempted takeoff from the Denver airport resulted in about the same fatalities. This green crew consisted of a captain who had only flown a few hours in the DC-9 he was flying, and a new copilot who had a miserable record of flying. This copilot had been released from several airlines because he couldn't pass any proficiency tests, either in a simulator or in an airplane. He had been hired by Continental because of his good looks and the impression he had made on management. Also, why had he been allowed to make the takeoff instead of the captain under these unfavorable conditions? Why did a simple gut feeling some fifty years before prevent such an accident from happening, whereas now, despite our modern knowledge, these things are still going on?

The DST, a version of the DC-3 converted into a sleeper at about that time, came up with some interesting happenings, a few of which I witnessed. After landing in Cleveland one night, I walked out of the plane and a lady clad in whatever peered out of the curtains to ask where we were. It took me a while to remember that it was Cleveland. On another occasion at Newark, I was walking up the aisle in the dark carrying my flight bags when I stepped on a foot sticking out into the aisle. The owner let out a yelp, banged his head against the top of his bunk, and was quiet thereafter.

On another sleeper flight from Chicago to Omaha some of my passengers elected not to avail themselves of their sleeping bunks and were being entertained in the lounge by none other than Eddie Peabody with his banjo. I strolled back through the cabin to listen to some of his music and it was great. That banjo sounded like a machine gun, only better, and in a humorous vein I asked him to render "The Flight of the Bumble Bee," knowing full well that this number was only for the violin of Jack Benny. Eddie rattled off the number so fast that it could have been a violin in action.

By this time I thought that the copilot who was flying the plane deserved to hear this classic, so I turned on the inner phone for his benefit. Returning to the cockpit I heard Omaha asking Chicago if they knew where that music was coming from. The clownish copilot had turned on the transmitter, and all of the western division operators were in on the concert. Later on Peabody married the stewardess on this flight.

One of the trips was a three-day go-around from Chicago to Newark, with several overnight sleepovers at the Cleveland dog-house. On this westbound segment we had Ham Lee aboard as a passenger. Ham was the dean of all airline pilots in the world, and had more flight time than anyone. But as a passenger he never knew what followed.

We encountered a thunderstorm midway in the flight, with a little turbulence, heavy rain and some lightning—nothing serious, but apparently upsetting to the copilot, who was a quiet but fine flight officer. Our uniforms were light gray and easily stained, and were supposed to last the full three days. The copilot was holding the flight log in his lap when suddenly he heaved his guts all over his trousers, the flight log on his lap and all over the cockpit, right down to the rudder pedals.

The stewardess was summoned and took one look at the scene and gasped "Oh, my God," then went back to the cabin to fetch some containers of water and wet towels to help us clean up the mess. We still had several days to go, so the copilot tried to wash and iron his trousers in the doghouse in Cleveland. A stewardess loaned him an electric iron to make them more pre-sentable, although they were still stained a little yellow. For the Cleveland to Chicago leg we changed crews, and the outbound captain, Al Tucker, was in a hurry as usual, so I didn't get a chance to tell him what had happened. Some time later, Al met me and asked what the hell had happened? The cockpit had been so foul he had had to fly all the way to Chicago with the cockpit windows open.

NOW that money was coming in, we decided to look for a house to buy. We found one in Western Springs for the elevated price of $8,000. It had an unfinished room upstairs, which would give me an opportunity to use my woodworking skills to advantage.

The town of Western Springs was small and was managed by

a businessman for one dollar per year. The chief of police became a friend, and anyone found walking on the street at night better have a good reason for being there. When we took our vacations, the chief periodically checked our house. A block away lived another pilot who shared my interest in fishing.

On one trip to New York I went out on a wild tuna fishing trip off Long Island. We wore ourselves out on this one, and the party hauled in about a ton of the big ones. My catch was three fish totaling 200 pounds—the largest of them weighing in at 90 pounds. I wasn't about to leave these beauties behind, so I flew the two largest fish home on my all-night trip with stops at Akron, Cleveland, Toledo and Chicago. The fish were in the rear cargo hold, and at each stop I ran around to the cargo pit to check on them. They were not iced, and after a while the passengers began to get wind of what I was doing and did a lot of chiding. Arriving home at about 3:00 A.M., I laid my catch on the front lawn and called my friend Jim Keaton, a real fisherman, to ask him to look at my catch. He came over in his pajamas to admire the loot. Normally a person would not appreciate getting a call at that hour just to be invited to look at some fish; but Jim was impressed.

I was just finishing the alterations and painting of our new house when a friend called with the news about Pearl Harbor. A few months later my orders came through to report for duty at Morrison Field, West Palm Beach. This was the second interruption of my happy times with United, and was to last four years.

Above: Chicago Midway Airport Control Tower.
Below: Boeing 40-B, used for checkout for air
transport rating. Fun stuff over Chicago, 1935.

Captain Charlie Peoples.
"You tell Air Traffic Control to go to hell!"

Dust storm over Nebraska, 1935.

CHAPTER 7
World War II

FIFTY AIR CORPS RESERVE OFFICERS from the major airlines were recalled to active duty after the bombing of Pearl Harbor. This group was known as Project 50 and was commanded
by Major Willis Proctor from American Airlines. We were pro-
cessed at Morrison Field, West Palm Beach, Florida, for our assignments to ATC bases around the world.

First of all came the physical exam, seemingly a necessity before any action started. By this time I am well versed in physical
exams and can spot an amateur examiner a mile away. To start
off I was told that I had turbinates in my nose, which was news
to me. Then I asked, "Now can I go home?" The reply was "absolutely not." Then came the eye test, and when I was told to
turn the knob until the dot lined up with the line I cranked and
cranked until the knob fell off but I couldn't get the two together.
The examiner blew his cork. He obviously hadn't mastered this
piece of equipment, because the line I was looking at was a crack
in the door into the room, and no amount of cranking could
have moved the crack in the door to line up with the dot. This
soldier went out for help and returned with an expert and the
two of them put the machine back together again. Had these
neophytes asked me, I could have shown them how to run a
physical exam from start to finish.

So far, except for the fact that a war was going on, things
weren't too bad, as I recall. My Aunt Mamie and Uncle Paul
lived in West Palm Beach and often invited me and my cohorts
to their home. We played poker, played the piano, sang songs
and had a good time. This war was beginning to look like a lot
of fun.

Aunt Mamie was an aircraft spotter as her wartime assignment, which required her to spot and report any hostile aircraft that might be a threat to the national security. One day she spotted an Italian bomber approaching the field from the south and promptly reported it to her boss. He told her to take another look-see, or at least have another cup of coffee. She stood her ground, and as things turned out this flying machine really was an enemy bomber. It had been captured by our forces and was being ferried back to the states for evaluation.

Fishing has always been my favorite sport, so I got in a little of it while waiting for my assignment to where I would begin my war service. One such trip off the West Palm Beach coast near the gulf stream was a classic. My wife and two other Air Corps wives and I chartered a boat to try for the sails. Uncle Paul recommended a skipper, and he was one of the best. The action started when two of the girls got hookups while I stood there and just watched. There was a lot of screaming, and one of the girls begged me to help her battle the monster, since she was violently ill and couldn't handle it anymore. The skipper went berserk trying to keep the two lines from crossing, which wasn't easy because these two apparently had no sense of direction.

Believe it or not, both sails were landed. Later that night Uncle Paul called me and asked, "What did you do to your skipper? I found him down at the local bar drunker than a skunk and mumbling something about three women hooked up with two sails at the same time."

I am on my way to my war assignment, which was to Santa Monica for the purpose of checking out the new Douglas C-54. Practice landings were made at the Long Beach airport. Johnny Sandow, also from Fort Crockett, and I were checking each other out on this mammoth bird, neither of us having the slightest idea about its characteristics. All we knew about it was how it looked when we saw it for the first time.

I tried the first landing and we selected ninety miles per hour as a good approach speed over the fence. This speed seemed adequate, since this plane was a little faster than its predecessor, the

DC-3. The crunching sound when we contacted the ground indicated that our estimate was on the short side, so we ad libbed a few more miles per hour and things turned out better. Sandy and I are not dummies, you know.

In the early days of the DC-4 almost every landing and take-off resulted in either a fuel leak or a hydraulic leak from some unit, making a puddle on the ground. Then it was up to the crew to determine which system was leaking. After one landing the co-pilot found a puddle under the wing and rubbed his hands in it and smelled it to determine which system was leaking. The crew chief came over and said, "Pardon me, sir, I've just taken a leak there."

After this temporary assignment some of us were assigned to Bolling Field, which was just across the Potomac from Washington, D.C. This outfit was a special mission group with an assortment of airplanes and ground equipment. The flight officers were recalled airline pilots with reserve commissions and were from all of the major airlines. The navigators were from the military and came right out of the top drawer. They not only could get you lost any place in the world, but could find your location at the drop of an octant. The crew chiefs were the best in the Air Corps.

The mission of this collection of aerial experience was to fly brass to any place in the world. Brass included high-ranking military officers, State Department officials, politicians, and even a president or two. Such names as Roosevelt, Truman, Wendell Wilkie, Davies the ambassador to Moscow and a movie of the treaty of surrender negotiated by General MacArthur and the Japanese on its flight to Washington appeared on our passenger and cargo lists.

These flights were not limited to domestic destinations; the globe was their field of operation. Our men dropped in at such out-of-the-way places as Africa, Europe, Russia, Siberia, Greenland, Iceland, South America, and most of the Pacific and Alaska. I can't think of a better assignment of war duty than this brass-hat squadron—except possibly the one a friend drew. He spent his duty time throughout the war as Navy captain of a gunboat equipped with one two-inch gun, with the responsibility of defending Tahiti from the Japanese. That assignment doesn't sound too bad either.

Here at Bolling Field the military traffic across the river to the Pentagon and Gravelly Point was heavy and was ferried by a Chriscraft power boat. One of the skippers attempting to master this boat was Gilbert Roland of the movies. He had trouble getting the hang of it, and the frustrated sergeant who was his coach was beside himself at times. On one of my trips across he approached the landing dock head on and knocked down a couple of Colonels with their briefcases who were waiting at the dock. As I recall, Roland was married to Constance Bennett and was the only buck private privileged to eat regularly at the commanding officer's table.

The desk awarded to me was labeled "Operations Officer" and stood in the middle of a small area which also had such tools of the trade as maps of every inch of the world as we knew it, several telephones (mostly for receiving traveling orders from across the Potomac) and a collection of crew members lounging about and exchanging jokes and fabrications about their past travels and waiting for their next flight to somewhere.

From this desk we assigned crews and planes to each mission and kept records of the status of everything that was going on— everything we knew about, that is. Some of the orders were top secret, and we were only told to fly to such and such place with a specific piece of equipment; who might be aboard was no business of ours.

The major decisions were made from the office next door, occupied by Major Willis Proctor, the group's C.O. A call from headquarters across the Potomac would describe the mission, and our office set up the crew and airplane. One such call came from President Roosevelt's office to the effect that Wendell Wilkie, who was returning from his round-the-world trip, would be delivered the following message as he approached Minneapolis. It read: "Under no circumstances will you discuss politics upon returning to this country." I delivered the message, and one can see how important my job was. One error on my part could have changed the history of the world. My performance was perfect.

Upon Mr. Wilkie's arrival, his loot and trophies were dumped on my office floor. The heap included sabers, rare maps, and gifts from many potentates around the world. Our group later staged an honor parade for Mr. Wilkie.

One of our craft was a C-87, which was a Liberator bomber converted to a passenger or cargo configuration. It was scheduled for a flight to Teheran with a few passengers aboard. I got a call from headquarters ordering me to make up a ramp so that one of the passengers would have an easy time stepping into the cabin. The step was about twelve inches high. At the other end of the phone was my old friend Charlie Skannal from Fort Crockett days, so I felt free to express my feelings on the matter. My words were "Why build a thing like that? Doesn't this bird know that there is a war going on?" Charlie answered firmly, "Build the ramp." Later I found out the passenger's name: Franklin Delano Roosevelt.

In any group there always seems to be a dry wit or a half one or a dim one. One of our navigators had such a one in Tom "Catfish" Williams, who had his share of the fun wit. Besides his regular octant he also carried a broken down instrument, and for fun purposes he would accidentally drop the thing on the floor, scattering parts all over in full view of the V.I.P. passengers. This was most effective when done over mid-ocean en route to some-where. It could also be dangerous to one's health, especially if your passengers lacked the basics of humor. But Catfish must have gotten by with this, because later he was ordered to flight training school by General Hap Arnold and became a pilot.

All of our pilots had to take a course in celestial navigation just in case the navigator became inoperative. In my practice sessions at Bolling I became fairly proficient at finding my location by using nothing more than the stars and the sun and an octant. With all due modesty I can say that I always found that I was somewhere near Washington D.C.

On one of my westbound flights across the south Atlantic I did a few practice celestials just to keep my hand in and to break up the monotony of the eleven-hour flight. I determined our locations on the map, but in each case they differed from the ones arrived at by the navigator. I was obviously rusty, so I let it go at that. The fly in the ointment was that my findings were correct; the navigator had been guessing our positions without bothering to use his octant and just marking them on the map.

Now, this kind of fraud is a no-no, especially when the skipper happens to be the commanding officer of this special mission squadron. Compare this with with the one mentioned earlier: the first became a pilot by command of General Arnold; the second was later court-marshaled for some civilian offenses.

A desk is not the same as a cockpit as far as a pilot is concerned. Purely by happenstance I assigned myself to a mission now and then, and they were all posh ones. Several trips to Nassau were not too unpleasant, and on these trips I got to visit my wife and daughter, who were still living in West Palm Beach.

My first mission out of the office was to Prestwick, Scotland and back by way of Goose Bay, Newfoundland, Greenland and Iceland. On stop one in Newfoundland I met Home McDowell, another United pilot recalled to active duty. He gave me my first glimpse of the new Jeep and offered to demonstrate its capabilities. We drove out into the forest, passing a fine moose on the way to a wide river which was flowing fairly fast.

Homer said that he had just crossed this river the day before with no sweat. This didn't look too good to me, so I offered to watch the demonstration from the bank, but he insisted that I go along. The Jeep went down into the water nose first, dunking the engine and almost dunking us.

Apparently this was not the same spot where Homer had made his first crossing. A tractor was brought in and the machine was hauled out of the river. I have had a lot of hours in a Jeep since then and it has served me well; but this first encounter bombed out.

On my return flight from Scotland I learned that Homer had

disappeared over Greenland and hadn't been located since. His emergency radio kept working for a long time, and he communicated with the base indicating that he was in good shape. The search team instructed him to fire off a flare at a designated time, which he did. The search plane flew directly over the spot, but no trace of his plane was ever found. This ice cap was a bear to fly over, the ice rising to 9000 feet in some places and the glare from the ice making the distinction between ice and sky almost impossible. There were others who were tooling along admiring the scenery when their bottoms suddenly got scraped and that was that.

The approach to the southern Greenland base runway must have been exciting to the many pilots who have landed there. This runway pointed directly at a mountain of ice, so there was no such thing as an aborted landing. You had your choice: either land or bore a hole in the wall of ice and rock. Takeoffs of course were in the opposite direction, and hopefully there would be no approaching aircraft to interfere with your departure. So we approached the arrival spot through icebergs and around the bend, all the time being assured by the control tower that no one was departing.

The next stop en route to Prestwick was Reykjavik, Iceland, and on landing we saw a wheel and a strut from an airplane lying on the runway. Later that night at the officers' club (where else?) I met with the new P-38 ace who had just shot down a German fighter whose wheel and strut had ended up on the runway. He related the circumstances of his kill, saying that when the enemy approached he scrambled up through the clouds, and just as he broke out of the overcast, the intruder appeared right in his line of sight, so he pulled the trigger. The facts of the war were now beginning to get through to me.

The leg from Iceland to Scotland and return to Iceland was routine, except that in Scotland I had my first taste of horse meat. All I can say about it is that it didn't bother me too much

As we were leaving Iceland for Greenland, one of our engines started to act cute, so we turned around in the clouds to return to Iceland. Our radio operator came forward and asked if we were turning around; he said Reykjavik had just requested information on what we were doing. After we landed I asked the operations officer how he knew that we had turned back. He smiled and said, "We have a way." It seems the British had a new experimental toy called RADAR.

Thence back again over the icebergs and on to Washington. At night over Maine we encountered a bunch of thunderstorms, with lightning all over the place. Our navigator left his post and crawled down into the plexiglass nose of the bomb bay to watch the fireworks. A bolt of lightning struck close to our nose, and the navigator came back up like a striped-fannied zebra and stayed in his station for the remainder of the trip.

Major General Ralph Royce, a colorful character dating back to World War I, chartered a mission to Salt Lake City by way of Cleveland, Chicago and North Platte on to Salt Lake. When we arrived at Cleveland we found that our B-23 had developed a need for a crucial engine part which we would have to have before we could proceed. The General saw a B-25 sitting in the hangar with the identical part we needed and decided to remove it from the B-25 so we could continue our flight. There was a kind of upheaval here, though, and we didn't get to rob this machine of its parts. As we found out later, the B-25 was involved in the atomic bomb project, which very few people knew about at that point in time, and not even a two-star general could override this one.

At North Platte some of our crew members went out to the Platte River to do a little duck hunting, which turned out to be so easy that a stone's throw could bring down a duck, and that we did.

Checking into the hotel in Salt Lake that evening, I opened my bag and found two of the ducks therein. It seems that the chief always has to be the butt of the best jokes. However we had the ducks prepared very nicely for dinner, courtesy of a delightful lady friend of one of the crew members.

Orders came down from headquarters that our group, with

its personnel and its air and ground equipment, would be transferred to another base. But what was left out of the orders was
the name of the base to which we were to move.

We contacted several bases with no luck, even though I made
it clear that we would only be tenants. I was beginning to feel
like a real homeless by that time, so I crossed the Potomac and
went to the Pentagon to contact Major Davenport Johnson of
Fort Crockett days. The friendships that had been created in the
Third Attack Group endured throughout World War II. But now
the major was a major general. He came out into the waiting
room and ushered me into his office, pausing long enough to ask
two colonels with their briefcases to please wait a while.

We had a cordial visit, discussing old times, and finally got
around to my problem. Various bases were discussed, with the
Billy Mitchell Field at Milwaukee being the most favorable from
our group's standpoint. The general said, "If you want it, you
can have it."

Time was of the essence, so the Tenth prepared to move. A
troop train was scheduled for our 1,000-man outfit and its
ground equipment to make the overnight trip to Milwaukee. I
promised the men that the trip would be made in luxurious comfort with all the amenities. The squadron boarded the train and I
gave the salute to the conductor to let her roll. The outside of the
train didn't look too promising, but the inside was even worse.
All the seats were old and even included some benches along the
windows. Fine coal dust permeated the floors and windows. In
short, it was the Wreck of the Hesperus on wheels.

Rolling out of the Washington depot we passed a posh, stain-
less steel passenger train that had pulled aside to allow us to
pass. The civilians were sitting in a comfy lounge; the dining cars
had the finest of linen and table settings, but we had military pri-
ority, so we passed them by.

Once we got out of the rail yards, this collection of cattle cars
picked up speed and roared toward our destination. At that
speed I fully expected the shingles to fly off. All commercial
trains were off to one side waiting for this military bullet to

zoom by, but by this time I was getting a little concerned, especially when the engineer didn't even slow down through the hills of Pennsylvania. Never before had I been worried about flying this close to the ground. At a pit stop for water I contacted the conductor and indicated that our military mission was not so urgent timewise, but arriving at our destination was. He understood, and away we went, just as fast as before, if not faster. I firmly believe that this engineer had been waiting for this chance to let her out and find out what she could do.

When we arrived at Milwaukee, a thousand men and officers disembarked happy as clams. But now I had to explain to the squadron why the trip hadn't quite come up to my promises. I delivered the most eloquent speech of my career, saying that I would request that "you men forget about our luxury train trip, and I want to commend you for a job well done." The laughter that followed this short speech assured me I had just gotten away with something.

As we settled into our new home we found the most friendly people ever gathered into one community. Every soldier who could make it into town could have a warm family of new friends. The several breweries welcomed us to their club facilities, and we threw a big parade downtown, with thousands of cheering spectators. The officers lived off the base in the Hotel Schraeder, and its bar was our officers' club.

Back in Washington we had a welter-weight boxer who was making a name for himself in the fight circles. He had also distinguished himself by being the only one in our outfit who had contracted V.D., and was therefore being detained in the guardhouse pending court martial. A number of us were attending a boxing match one evening, and much to our surprise our man in the guardhouse climbed over the ropes to do his thing. This called for some further investigation.

Years later, after the war, I saw his name featured in a boxing match in Denver, and being interested I dropped in on the event, stopping by his dressing room where he was preparing for the bout. When I approached him he jumped to attention and saluted while his trainer kept trying to calm him down. After a minute or two in the first round he went down for the count. I've always felt a little guilty about that night.

A CALL came from higher up requesting that our newly acquired C54 also be used for checking out a certain Lt. Col. Paul Tibbetts in the heavier plane. He had been the pilot for General Eisenhower in Europe, but regs are regs, so I checked him out—a mere formality, since he could have stepped into the C-54 and flown it anywhere without any outside help.

Tibbetts told me he was going to try to transfer me from the Air Transport Command to a new B-29 group being organized at Salt Lake, which he would command. A month later I received a letter from him saying that my command would not release me.

A year later, while I was in Naples, Italy, I learned that Col. Paul Tibbetts was the skipper of the *Enola Gay,* which had ruined Hiroshima.

We received a request from the Douglas Aircraft Company to show off this new monstrous bird to their employees at the assembly plant north of Chicago, the site of the future O'Hare Airport. The employees had never seen the finished product which they were assembling. The runway was still in the early stages of construction; the concrete had been poured, but the edges had not yet been filled in. At this point it looked like the Great Wall of China with heavy construction equipment scattered around it. The plan was for our C-54 to leave Milwaukee after all of the construction machinery was moved away from the runway and land at Chicago to show the employees their work of art.

I made several passes over the new runway with the landing gear both retracted and extended, plus a few extra didoes for the benefit of the huge crowed that assembled for the viewing. After the landing they inspected the craft. This may have been the first landing at Chicago O'Hare Airport, even before it was built.

Our twenty-three-piece band and the squadron staged a review for the commanding general of the area. His aide, a Major King, standing by me, seemed very excited about the band. He would point out "there is so and so" every so often and apparently knew many of our band members. Small wonder, for he was Major Wayne King.

Now we had new orders to transfer the outfit to La Guardia Airport. On this squadron move I chickened out on the train ride and flew a plane instead. I found the troop train on its way eastward and flew past the coach windows in a passing salute, and that is a dirty trick.

I returned to Milwaukee to pick up my family, and ran into gas rationing. I was given enough gas to drive to New York, with little or no reserve for finding a place to live. In my search for an apartment on Long Island, I passed Coney Island, which was jammed with parked cars. I hope they were not all looking for a place to live, or maybe they just lived there on the beach.

After getting settled down I drew a mission away from the desk to fly the first Fireball Express, which was to take a C-87 loaded with much-needed parts for the lads flying the "Hump" from India into Kunming. Up until now most of the parts going that way had been waylaid along the way, so that few if any arrived where they were needed most. Each base commander was tempted to help himself to these parts in order to solve his maintenance problems. By command of General George, no base commander along the way would remove any of the parts for his own use. This worked well all the way to Agra, India, and the parts arrived untouched.

On this trip I brought along a few cases of spirits to dispense to my friends along the way. The first stop in Africa was at Accra, where I met an old UAL friend and offered him a bottle of the spiritual stuff. He thanked me and took me to a tent nearby in which was stashed all kinds of the stuff in copious quantities.

Maduigera was the next stop, and on the landing approach a good-sized thunderstorm was in progress. Looking down as we circled we could see scores of wildebeest and zebras milling around apparently in panic because of the weather or because of our airplane or both. After landing we learned that a particular

giraffe stationed nearby had found out that C-rations were tasty
and that if you stuck your head into the cockpit window of any
C-47 passing through you would get a handout, and the crews
always seemed to be more than happy to share their rations with
this animal.

Some crews passing through for the first time might have been
startled by the huge head of this giraffe. After all, the head of
this animal must have looked about the size of a whale as it appeared in the window. I drove a C-87 and didn't get this greeting
from the giraffe, probably because my windows were too low for
him to do his mooching.

Aden, Arabia came up next, offering a rest stop and some
much-needed sleep. I was awakened by a British officer with a
flashlight who demanded an explanation of why we were flash-
ing signals to the enemy fleet nearby. This must have been due to
our crew chief, who went down into the wheel well with a flashlight to see if the landing gear was down and locked. I told the
Britisher to get lost and went back to sleep.

When landing at Aden we developed a propeller problem, and
out on the desert floor in pitch darkness our crew chief had scattered parts all over the sand.

The password of the day was "Jeep," and I went out in the
dark of night to see how things were going. I met up with a sen-
try who was as black as the Arabian Nights. I found myself with
a bayonet pointed at my belly and a set of white teeth shouting
something. It took quite a while before I could remember "Jeep."

The crew chief finally assembled the propeller mess, and we
were on our way to Misara, just off Saudi Arabia, passing over
the Queen of Sheba's burning sands of Hadramaut. Misara island
is a flat piece of land inhabited by a large population of antelope.
The next landing was at Karachi, where we roamed the streets
taking in the sights of camels, donkeys and other traffic hazards.
It was there that a cute little girl gave us a friendly smile and said
"You go to hell." Some G.I.s must have been there before us.

The end of the line was Agra, India, where we delivered our
much-needed parts to the Hump operation. Our crew did a little

sightseeing to the Taj Mahal aboard a two-wheeled sulky powered by a very scrawny horse. Occasionally the horse did his
thing, and the driver picked up some straw from under our feet
and wiped him. As we passed a large pond we saw a youngster
relieving himself in the water while numerous other people were
drinking out of the same pond, which also had a water buffalo
standing in the middle. This was my first impression of the sanitary conditions in India.

The Taj must be the most magnificent structure in the world,
but when I saw it the dome was being cleaned and had scaffolds
over it, so my pictures were not the best. The long, shallow moat
in front of the Taj was about eight inches deep, and another impression came to my mind. Richard Haliburton, of travel fame,
has traveled the world and swam in such places as the
Hellespont, the Dardanelles, and other bodies of water as well as
in the moat in front of the Taj Mahal. He must have been a good
surface swimmer, considering the depth of the moat.

At the hotel in Agra Bill Arthur gave me a call and told me he
would be riding with me back to the U.S. Bill was head of operations for Air Transport Command in Washington. He had been
sent to India to find out why the C-46s were always losing
power at altitude when leaving Agra for Kunming. He found out
soon enough when his engine quit and he went overboard via the
parachute and landed in a valley that was only 14,000 feet above
sea level. He also lost his fine collection of pipes in the process.

Coming back with Bill aboard via the south Atlantic we
stopped at Belim, at the mouth of the Amazon River, and I went
into town to have a little recreation. I dropped into a likely place,
which seemed to be a frivolous night club with music and all of
the trimmings. A military police sergeant confronted me and said
that this was an enlisted men's whorehouse and that he would
have to take me in. Since I was the commanding officer of a
1,000-man squadron of enlisted men and officers, this was a
most embarrassing situation. But at that point another non-com
walked up and told the MP to lay off—this is a personal friend
of our commanding officer.

This was not the end of the Belim venture. I went shopping for some mosquito boots in the local marketplace, where a very attractive young lady approached me and said, "You and me, two dollahs." I replied that I didn't understand, and she repeated "You and me, two dollahs." I countered by saying "I no comprende."

Just then Bill Arthur came around the corner, just as the lady said, "No comprende, Jesus Christ."

When we came back to the airport to continue our flight home, we found that our C-87 had been stripped of its contents and passenger seats had been installed. This was contrary to the command of General George, who had said that no base commander would remove any of the contents of our plane—and that meant both going and coming. I went storming into the office of the Priorities and Traffic officer, a captain who determines what goes on each flight out of his station, and I reminded him of my orders, but he said that he would decide what would go aboard my aircraft and that a group of soldiers returning to the U.S. would be aboard.

Getting nowhere with this executive, I had to contact the base commander for some action. He knew all about the special orders, and within minutes there was a lot of activity around our C-87. The seats were removed and the cargo put back on the plane, and we were on our way back to New York, mission accomplished.

On the next mission I became a mail man, this time around the north Atlantic, through Newfoundland to Prestwick, Scotland, thence on to North Africa, Natal, South America and home. The first leg went well until we arrived at Prestwick and were diverted to another aerodrome somewhere in Wales because of weather. Some forty years later, on a trip through the area, I tried to find this alternate airport, but no one seemed to know anything about it. Perhaps it has been plowed under.

Next, on St. Mawgan at Land's End at the bottom tip of England, our approach was interrupted by two flares shot up, which was the signal to do a go-around because a wounded fighter plane was coming in for a landing.

On our departure we were instructed to maintain absolute radio silence throughout the flight until we reached Marrakech in Africa, and that we did.

Just off Brest, France, which was held by the Germans, we were flying just a few feet above the water in the darkness when we went right down the deck of a German destroyer sitting there dead in the water. Radio silence prevented us from relaying his position, but later that night the destroyer was sunk by the British. I'll always wonder what went on in the minds of the crew of the destroyer when an enemy plane flew over their deck in the fog.

AFTER delivering the mail we had to return to the U.S. with whatever cargo could be put aboard. Out of Marrakech we had on board a bunch of rocks that were yellowish and bluish in the cargo hold. Rocks and gems are one of my hobby interests, but these were from Dullsville. They looked even less likely to be important military cargo. Perhaps they were autonite, a uranium ore that sometimes has a yellowish and bluish coloring, and they could have been the start of the nuclear age.

Things went well on this flight except that out of Natal in South America one engine quit cold. We decided to land at Fortaleza to correct the problem. We were above heavy clouds, which meant letting down through unknown weather to land at the airport, which was at sea level. Before dipping my nose into the clouds I studied my map and noticed that there were a lot of high mountains below. As usual I made a lucky decision and headed out to sea for the descent. No sensible pilot wants to run into a bunch of rocks while he is flying in the clouds.

I was still hoping to get home for Christmas, and fortunately a new engine arrived just in time for us to continue the flight home.

Leaving Puerto Rico for New York a hurricane was in progress in the New York area, and when we were just about over the infamous Bermuda Triangle on our way with no problems except for heavy rain and a little lightning we got a call from Miami operations directing us to return to Miami. My first reaction to this summons was to radio back telling them to go fly their own kite, since I was a command pilot, but I relented and headed for Miami. There was no reason why we could not have continued on to New York, but I caved in.

SOONER or later everyone gets upgraded or downgraded somewhere along the way. This time I was transferred out of my favorite assignment with the Special Mission Squadron to a higher echelon, the domestic headquarters of the Air Transport Command, located on Wall Street just across the street from the stock exchange.

My first attempt to report for duty was to try to drive my car from Long Island to the offices. I had to call in and admit that I couldn't make it because I had gotten hopelessly lost in the maze of New York City traffic. The next day was not much better after an abortive effort to get to the new headquarters by way of the subway. I ended up in Brooklyn, and when I came up out of the tube there were only a few buildings of a lower order and none of the skyscrapers I had expected. Although this was no way to make a favorable impression on the boss, I finally did report for duty.

Air Transport Command occupied the entire seventeenth floor of the building and was staffed by military and civilian employees, and as assitant chief of staff, operations, I got settled in. Two able secretaries, Amy and Marie, did noble work for me, and I often wondered if they were really running the show.

There were still some adventures to be had from this lofty office. Our cadre of airplanes at La Guardia Airport consisted of a couple of C-47s and some B-23s. One day I got a call from our engineering officer telling me that a mechanic had stolen one of our C-47s, taken off and made a couple of sweeps at the control tower and finally bounced to an abrupt halt in a heap. The conversation preceding this maneuver had been between two mechanics, one of whom said "I bet I can fly this thing," and the other bet he couldn't. He did fly it, but my immediate problem was to explain to headquarters what had happened, and it wasn't easy. The simple explanation that one of our mechanics had stolen one of our airplanes and scared everybody to death sounded hollow and tinny, but it was the best I could come up with.

My secretary, Amy, came in one day and excitedly said that there was a C-47 just down the street with its nose into the side of a building. I walked over and, sure enough, there was the fighter with its nose buried in the side of the building.

There were numerous administrative flights out of this headquarters to conduct our mission. One covered the string of ATC bases throughout Central America. Our commanding officer and his deputy accompanied us on this inspection tour. The border was crossed at Laredo, Texas, where we received our medical briefing on the dangers of V.D. as required by regulations when leaving the country. This was done at a local bar, and while the flight surgeon droned on and on with his lecture I noticed a tall Texan sitting with highball in hand and listening to these goings on. He then interrupted and said, "And you can't get it by radio, either."

In Mexico City we visited a bull fight, and our C.O., who had a few belts ahead of time, began to shout, "Kill the toreador! Hooray for the bull!" He was escorted out of the arena by the police. It seems that rooting for the bull is just not done in Mexico.

My copilot on this trip was George Rodiak, an adventurer in his own right. At a meeting with some locals farther south in Nicaragua, George and another man kept staring at each other until all of a sudden the other blurted out, "You are the one who flew us out of the field when the Sandinistas were coming at us from out of the woods!"

We had occasion to fly over the ruins of Monte Alban and Mitla, so we dipped low and circled several times for a close look. The deputy commander sent word up to the cockpit that he was having a heart attack and to stop all of this fooling around, and so on we went.

After landing in Managua, Nicaragua, we checked into a hotel and while we were watching a bicycle race an American General Bartlett accosted us and asked what we were doing there. He said he would have our bags picked up at the hotel and we would be quartered at his mansion. Next came the review with the parade of troops, and as soon as that was over we would enjoy his hospitality.

Some time later in New York General Bartlett showed up at my office with a letter from General Hap Arnold saying that we should show this officer every courtesy. From the tone of the letter it sounded like he was about to ask for our fleet of airplanes or something similar, but all he wanted was to hitch a ride to Dallas on one of our transports.

In Guatemala our C.O. and his deputy decided to leave us and proceed to Panama on Braniff Airlines. Apparently they didn't like our brand of flying, especially at Oaxaca, where we circled low to inspect the ruins, and they felt they would be safer on the airline.

When we landed at Panama none other than the commanding officer and his deputy were waiting for us at the flight line, ready and eager to rejoin us for the rest of the trip. It seems that on their landing in Costa Rica they had been scared out of their wits. The field was short, and after a series of bounces and abortive attempts the pilot finally got it down. So they were pleased to take a chance with us, and not another peep was heard thereafter.

THE big transfer from my domestic duties to a foreign base resulted in an assignment to ATC headquarters in London, England. While waiting for this transfer my wife and I went skiing at Split Rock, New York, where I made a stupid attempt to try a slope covered with ice. I wondered at the time why there were no other skiers around, but I took off and broke a few speed records down the slope. An ankle was fractured and a kneecap split so I reported to headquarters in London on crutches.

I requested a warmer climate for my assignment and was sent to Naples, Italy to be the operations officer for the Mediterranean area, including such spots as London, Paris, Marseilles, Cairo, Athens, Crete, Algiers, Budapest, Bucharest, Sofia, Belgrade and all of the stops around the Mediterranean. This was to be my new camping ground for the duration.

Arriving in Naples I saw the beautiful flowers, orange trees and other flora found in tropical climes and also a typhoid epidemic going on. Funeral processions were parading down the street in droves with their ornate hearses drawn by pairs of plumed horses.

For my billet I drew a nice apartment within walking distance of the ATC officers' club. It was owned by a Miss Rita Firpo, Italy's leading movie actress at that time. Her apartment was loaded with scrapbooks, fine paintings, a beautiful grandfather clock—and *bed bugs!* On my first night there the bed started to crawl around as I tried to get some sleep, and even the pillows moved. This was a night of horrors for me, but the next day the club officer and his men eradicated the scourges.

From then on the place was livable—up to a point. Sometimes the elevator would stop cold between floors, and if it stopped at the wrong place one would have to crawl out and risk being cut in two should it start up again.

In the Naples bathroom there was a piece of equipment unfamiliar to me. It looked like a toilet seat but squirted water all over the place when turned on. I concluded that whatever its designed use may have been, it would be best utilized as a beer cooler, and so it became my beer chiller for the duration—and a good one I may add. Later I found out that this was a bidet, to be used as a substitute for the old corn cob, the Sears catalog, or ordinary toilet paper.

A young Italian housekeeper went with the apartment, and there were several during my tenure in Naples. Some wanted to wash and iron my socks and other clothing as well as performing other duties, but the main idea was that Uncle Sam was providing me with comfortable quarters quite unlike the old hangar dog houses that United had furnished us in the early years at Cleveland and other terminals. Whatever inconveniences there may have been, it was still better than the tents of the troops who were doing the real fighting.

The back bedroom was used for my darkroom, where I could continue my hobby of photography, taking pictures and developing same.

One night, out of the blue, Rita Firpo in person showed up at the door. She was disheveled and in tatters, rather small of stature and ordinary-looking. She told me that the night before a soldier had demanded favors in exchange for a pass to freedom. She wanted to stay the night here in her apartment in the back bedroom.

I tried to explain to her that the bedroom had been converted to a darkroom and that in no way could she stay there. I contacted the club officer, who arranged to have her stay with an Italian family living in the same apartment building. The next day she showed up in the lobby clean and well-dressed in white, and after that I never saw her again. Why do my friends stare at me when I tell them this story? Am I missing something?

The flight officers were assembled for a preliminary briefing about the plans for carrying out my assignment. There had been reports of pilferage of the pain-killing drugs contained in the emergency kit of each cockpit. Also there had been some questionable activities in the exchange of expensive furs and jewelry in Copenhagen and other spots. But my message was clear and to the point: I would go along with any honest mistake and stand by each and every one of them if they kept their noses clean, and when their tour of duty was up they would be rotated back to the states in good order. On the other hand, I promised to torpedo the man who thought he could get around the system. I believe that message got through to some extent.

Ironically a year later, just before my own tour was over, one of our pilots on a flight to Athens dove on a fishing boat, struck the mast and went in, eliminating his crew and the aircraft. That's a hard way to cut short your tour of duty.

Many officers and men pulled off this Naples operation, too many to mention them all, but a few were Brandy Brandenburg,

Stan Middleton, Jack Tarr and Louis Illioff from operations and
Lieutenant Young from maintenance.

This military airline turned out to be entirely different from
the one at the domestic division of ATC. We were prohibited
from flying between the Balkan nations, and each flight had to
start from Naples and return to Naples.

Further stipulations by the communists required that we not
only specify the names of the crew members but also the serial
numbers of the aircraft two weeks in advance. The listing of
crew members by name was fairly simple, but to list the exact serial number of each plane was virtually impossible for maintenance reasons. We got around this obstacle by painting a number
on each plane with water-based paint, which could easily be
washed off after the flight. The system went smoothly, and I
prided myself that I pulled a fast one on the Russkies.

Matyasfold Airport out of Budapest was a small dirt field just
about big enough to accommodate a C-47 under favorable conditions, one of which was furnishing the pilot some indication of
the wind direction and velocity, namely a wind sock. There was
none, and when I announced my intention to hang up a wind
sock I was told that it would not be permitted and that "you
Americans are just trying to take over the airport." To make sure
that the wind sock would be installed I flew it over there myself
and had it put in place. Nothing further happened, and we had
our wind sock and landings and takeoffs became easier. Perhaps
this simple trait of the Russians might be considered when our
country's leaders deal with them.

Another one of our Balkan terminals, at Belgrade, Yugoslavia,
was in need of a few drums of gasoline to refuel our returning
aircraft. I received a cable from Marshall Tito informing me that
there would be dire results if we attempted to bring in any fuel
for our aircraft. This was of zero concern to us since we knew
that Tito had nothing in the way of military means to carry out
his threat. We delivered the drums of fuel, and nothing more
happened.

Our base at Naples was on the receiving end of several

groups of visitors, some undesirable and others of the more welcome type.

A hundred German prisoners of war were assigned to the base, and we were told to take care of them. They were all healthy young blond men, militarily exact and up to snuff. A small area was set aside for them and they were told that this would be their home away from home for the duration. Enjoy. They were given the necessary tools and tents and they went to work. Latrine trenches were dug, the camp was laid out, tents were erected and their camp was complete by nightfall, which impressed me quite a bit.

After their camp was set up, they moved on to earning their keep, which included many duties around the base, one of which was to maintain the sanitary conditions around the operations office. While walking in the dark corridor one day I stumbled over one of them who was mopping the floor. He jumped to attention and startled me a bit. I told him never to do that again, and he never did.

Other visitors included Leon Blum, former premier of France, and his entourage. Our instructions were to greet them on their arrival and give them the VIP treatment. So we field-grade officers welcomed them with a movie- and picture-taking arrival. Why they had been sent to our base at Capodachino was not told to us, except that they were a cut above the German prisoners we had already inherited.

Colonel Nels David, assistant chief of staff for the Mediterranean region, had his office in downtown Naples, and as director of operations at Capodichino we made many inspection trips throughout the region. On one such flight with Col. David we were to fly Mr. and Mrs. Jacobs, the new consul and his wife, and several members of his staff to Tirano, Albania. After landing we reached his office by way of a parade of limousines, with spectators along the way waving American flags and shouting "Tru-man! Tru-man! President Tru-man!" At the consulate we were given a banquet fit for a potentate and out of my class as a lieutenant colonel in the Air Corps.

Brigadier General Jerry Lee, from Fort Crockett days, was stationed at Bari, Italy, just across the peninsula from Naples. He dropped in at our base now and then and would startle my operations people by asking, "Where is that SOB boss of yours?"

Jerry was a rough-and-ready character, a football player from Texas A&M, and he was all man. In Rome he clobbered a visiting congressman who criticized him for tooling around in a staff car at taxpayers' expense. Shortly afterward he was transferred to a base in Nebraska.

Munich was one of our terminals and had its share of war-induced carnage, with much of the city in ruins, including Hitler's own beer hall, where his skullduggery got its start. The cleanup of this rubble had not yet gotten under way, with the downtown area being littered with goods from the various shops and ripe for looters. Outside one building two G.I.s with machine guns passed me and commented that there were a couple of S.S. troops inside. After a few minutes two machine gun bursts seemed to end that story.

Outside of Munich was Dachau, a beautiful little village with red-tile roofs and tree-lined streets that reminded me of Palos Verdes Estates in California. The adults there were cold and seemingly unaware that one of the most notorious torture camps of the Nazi regime was right in their own backyard. But the kids were always smiling and greeted us warmly, not yet having gotten into the spirit of this conflict.

The camp at Dachau had just been occupied by the Americans and remained intact, just as it had been when captured. Fun-loving G.I.s were lifting the girls' skirts to dust them with DDT in an effort to stem the plague of pants bunnies that were running amok under these camp conditions.

We were taken around the compound by a former member of the staff, and he pointed out the gruesome details without any show of embarrassment or guilt. He could well have been a docent showing us through a museum.

The special torture given to male inmates was explained in detail, and the racks and ditches were pointed out. The men were hung up on a scaffold and their testicles jiggled with sticks while a bunch of vicious dogs made short work of their private parts. But the torturers were at least considerate enough to shoot them afterward and dump their carcasses into a ditch.

The ovens used for the disposal of victims were startling enough. Children got no special treatment, and I saw a tiny finger or two among the ashes.

The ashes were returned to the surviving relatives in gallon-sized urns that had been filled with a shovel from the ash pits of the ovens. All that the relatives could be sure of was that someone's ashes were in the urns, but whose no one will ever know.

It was absolutely unbelievable that a so-called human being could ever cook up this slate of tortures. We were glad to leave this cesspool.

At Munich-Reim Airport we got a glimpse of the first wartime jet fighter, which had given our allies a bit of trouble when it first entered the fray. One of the engineers who had worked on the design of this jet was on hand to explain the features of this new war machine.

Hitler's Eagle's Nest, close by Munich, was reached by a narrow, winding mountainous road through several tunnels. The main nest was a camp high up in the mountains with barracks for the soldiers and officers and Hitler's main residence, which was a luxurious domicile with all the amenities, including radiant heat. The view from the living room was magnificent. The kitchen and baths were the most modern of the time. But all of this had just been messed up by the British bombers, and remained just as they had left it.

But the underground city at the very top was the most impressive of all. A bronze door opening to an elevator took Hitler and friends to the top layout, and in case the elevator broke down, a long path was also available. The elevator was not working when we visited, so we took the path up. The underground complex had been somewhat shot up by the occupying G.I.s, who had machine-gunned most of the rooms when they took over.

By "city" I mean that Hitler had a complete dental office and medical facilities, living quarters and everything else to live in style underground like a gopher. Eva Braun had her own suite here, and it looked pretty luxurious to me, with all of the necessary feminine requirements for existence at the top level.

There were a number of framed paintings owned by Hermann Goering that had been slashed by knives and taken away by the Americans, which was unfortunate.

UP to now I felt that my military obligations to the country had been fulfilled to the best of my ability considering my age, experience and capabilities. However, in Naples I received a draft-board notice that was mailed to me from Western Springs, putting me on notice that unless I reported in at once they would come and get me. So I guess I'm a draft dodger, although no one ever showed up.

The Andrews Sisters—Patty, LaVerne and Maxine—visited our Naples outpost and gave out with some nice singing for the G.I.s One of our apartments had a grand piano, and with the piano and the sisters some of us enjoyed some great music. Looking out the window one evening I saw a crowd of Italians gathered around and enjoying the music, as most Italians do. Among the classics rendered that evening were "Take it Off, Take it Off, Cried a Voice in the Rear" and "Lili Marlene." One little girl with an accordion did "Lili Marlene," and it was of the best.

Some time before, on a trip to Budapest, I had made arrangements for a local lady to custom-make two dolls dressed in the local costumes, which I wanted to give to my two granddaughters on my return to the states. Patty came up to my apartment, saw the dolls and wanted them at all costs. I kept the dolls and resisted all attempts to take them from me.

The Andrews Sisters' last performance before hundreds of the military was going strong when word came in that the war was over. It was an emotional moment for all. Patty was given the news backstage and asked to deliver the glad tidings to her audience. Her voice was quivering as she made the announcement, and the rest of the evening's program did not follow the original script, and ended up in a happy conglomerate of entertainment, with everybody taking part.

By this time it becomes apparent that I am not a real war hero, and as far as I know, the first and only time I was shot at was the day after the war ended, while I was flying through the Brenner Pass en route to Munich. Small arms fire and rifle bursts came at me from both sides of the pass. Apparently the locals had not yet gotten the word.

For me things happened fast after that. It was my time to go home, as it was for most of us. I was offered two choices, either ferry a war-weary B-17 back to the states, or assume the position of air attaché to the U.S. embassy in Bucharest, Romania, in which case I would automatically be promoted to full colonel. The choice was easy, and I selected to go home with the B-17, since I was getting a little homesick and was eager to see my family.

I crewed my B-17 with several members of the staff, and homeward bound we went on probably the happiest flight of my life. After flying over Africa and South America we touched down at West Palm Beach, the same spot where I had started this war business four years before.

Every one of us was greeted as a hero. Apples, cookies and other goodies were given out by American girls, who never looked better. Even as we walked around the streets it was apparent that we were home. But looking back now I can't help thinking about some of the returnees from Viet Nam and Korea and the way they were treated in some cases. We were the lucky ones.

Now I am again a train commander, with about a thousand officers and men who were returning to Fort Sam Houston in San Antonio, Texas for processing back to civilians. I'm a bird man at heart, and I keep wondering why I always ended up in charge of a train. On the ride to San Antonio we stopped for a short time somewhere in the middle of Mississippi, where our men spotted a cold beer stand and they rushed to quench their thirst left over from the war. The jerks selling the beer knew that these men were likely patsies, and peddled the bottles at an exorbitant price. The soldiers, who were just returning from taking care of the real enemy, were about to take these racketeers apart. I had to remind them that it would be a better idea if we didn't botch it up at this late stage by taking on a couple of two-bit cons.

We made it through this one and arrived at Fort Sam Houston for the final red tape, which was the only red tape I've ever really enjoyed. I met my wife at the fort and drove to Tyler, Texas, where my daughter was staying, and then on to Chicago, where we planned to move back into our house, which had been temporarily rented out.

*Above: Thanksgiving dinner, 10th Transport Squadron;
Maj. Carl Recknagel and Maj. Gen. Harold George.
Below: The crew of the first Fireball Express,
NewYork–Agra, India, 1943.*

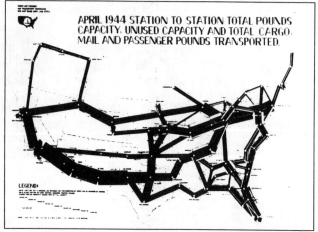

Above: Special Missions Group, Lt. Col. Willis Proctor, commanding; Headquarters Squadron, Maj. Ralph Read, commanding; 10th Transport Squadron, Maj. Carl Recknagel, commanding. Below: Domestic division routes, Air Transport Command; Lt. Col. Carl Recknagel, assistant chief of staff, Operations.

MARCH 1943

Flew Willkie and Standley, Now They Fly From Here

They fly Wendell Willkie around the world and transport members of the Roosevelt party to Casablanca. They take ambassadors and generals to Moscow. They flew supplies to embattled Bataan and Java and evacuated pilots and key personnel. They chart air routes over the Congo jungles and then carry in the parties to carve out landing fields and supply bases.

They are members of the air transport command group which has taken over Milwaukee's Gen Mitchell field as a headquarters and operations base. You may have passed them on the street and you may meet them—unless they are off on another trip to South America or Africa or Asia.

* * *

Pipe smoking, laconic Maj. Carl E. Recknagel at 36 is commanding officer of the group's 10th ferrying squadron, key unit of the transport command. Over the silver wings above his left breast pocket is the star of a senior army pilot, awarded on a basis of hours flown and years of service. A product of the army air corps' rigorous training, he won his wings at Kelly field, Texas, in 1928 and served two years with the 3rd attack group before resigning from active duty to join United Air Lines. With United for nine years, he flew the New York-Salt Lake run, making his home in Chicago. He admits that he "sometimes flies along with the boss." To them he is "the squarest C. O. in the business." He is married and the father of one daughter.

* * *

Navigator for Wendell Willkie on his globe circling tour was Capt. John C. Wagner, 27, who terms the former Republican presidential candidate "a mighty fine boy to fly with." With Willkie, he met Stalin and attended the famous banquet at the Kremlin. Members of the plane crew included Master Sergt. James M. Cooper, Staff Sergt. Victor P. Minkoff and Sergt. Charles H. Reynolds, all of whom are stationed at Gen. Mitchell field.

Before that tour, Capt. Wagner made a "routine" flight to Australia and wound up helping with the evacuation from Java. Airfields that were under Japanese attack all day were the night landing points for the big transports.

The captain won air medals for the evacuation work and the Willkie tour. He is unmarried.

* * *

Twice winner of the distinguished flying cross is dark, smiling Capt. Theodore J. Boselli. Like Wagner, he is 27, a graduate of Pan American Airways' first navigation class at Miami and a member of the transport command since shortly after it was organized in 1941 as the ferrying command.

Modestly, he says he won the first DFC for being a member of the first transport flight to cross the north Atlantic. The second was for charting the course for the Hurricane mission to Moscow, and the third for helping evacuate fliers from the hell on Bataan. His was the last plane to leave Mindanao airport before the peninsula fell. He has flown MacArthur, Wavell, Spaatz and Chennault.

His wife is a nurse in Florida.

* * *

"Daddy" to the group's enlisted personnel is Master Sergt. Robert B. Norris, who at 53 will leave soon on furlough, after which he expects to be commissioned and return to the group here. He has been in the Army 30 years and fought through four major World war engagements. Fifteen years ago he was transferred to the air corps. As hangar chief, the stocky sergeant supervises all engine changes and "hunts down the gremlins."

Norris' deepest regret is that he had to turn down Gen. Jimmy Doolittle's bid to go along on the Tokyo raid because he could not be spared by his squadron.

* * *

A flier since he was 17, Capt. Joe Kimm at 31 has flown more than one and three-quarter million miles, and is "happy that I have the experience behind me to do this job." As a pilot for Northwest Airlines, Inc., he flew through Milwaukee regularly in peacetime.

Capt. Kimm has been to "only a few places — the regular spots like South America, Africa and India," and he can't see much difference between flying a civilian plane for Northwest and a transport for the army. "We just go a little farther," he says, "and fly over more water."

The captain's wife and two children live in Minneapolis.

* * *

When Capt. William B. Hicks, 28, climbed aboard the plane he was to navigate in Casablanca, he had no idea that the passengers were members of the Roosevelt party and that the chief executive also was bound for Africa on another plane.

That trip was uneventful—unlike the trip to Russia with the Gen. Bradley mission when the oil lines of the big transport froze and the pilot crash landed in the deep snow blanketing a Siberian airport.

"A little bit of everything," is the way the captain describes his transport command experience. He was with the party that surveyed the air route over the Congo, and seven days later he was in Ireland.

His wife is with him here at their Knickerbocker hotel apartment.

* * *

Capt. Robert G. Polhamus, 30, who comes from Seattle, Wash., says he has never had a close call in ten years of flying, "because I don't believe in 'em." A graduate of Stanford university and Kelly field, he served in the air corps three years before becoming a Northwest Airlines pilot between Seattle and Billings, Mont.

He flew Admiral Standley to Russia to take over the duties as ambassador.

The captain's wife and their twin sons, aged 3, live in Palo Alto, Calif.

* * *

Master Sergt. James A. McVicar, 28, has been in the ATC since it was organized. He enlisted in 1935 and got his training at Chanute field, Illinois. Now senior radio operator, he keeps the radio equipment in tune and conducts "brushup courses to keep pilots and radio men up on Morse code and the various signals which Pan American Airways, the RAF, the French and other nationality groups use.

Yes, he has been in on "quite a few things" with Boselli on the evacuation flights from the Philippines, and was a member of a crew that took off personnel from Java.

"What difference does it make whether you hang your hat in India or Australia?" he asks. The sergeant is single.

Maj. Carl E. Recknagel

Capt. John C. Wagner

Capt. Theodore J. Boselli

Sergt. Robert B. Norris

Capt. Joe Kimm

Capt. William B. Hicks

Capt. Robert G. Polhamus

Sergt. James A. McVicar

Above: Munich, the beer hall where it all started.
Below: Mr. Jacobs, ambassador to Albania, Mrs. Jacobs and staff.

Above: The aerodrome, Tirana, Albania.
Below: Parade into Tirana.

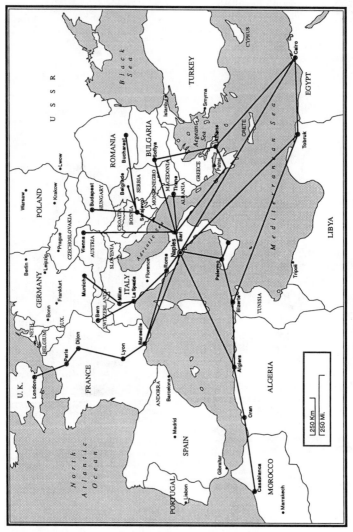

The Mediterranean operation.

Above: Lt. Archer with Russian wacsky, Sofia, Bulgaria, 1944.
Below: The staff at Capodachino.

Above: Tiger tank, Munich.
Below: Urns at Dachau for the ashes of cremated victims to be
sent home to relatives.

THE STARS AND STRIPES

Officers? No, Never!--Well, Hardly Ever

On Aug. 22, The Stars and Stripes carried an Army News Service dispatch from New York which said in part:

"The three [Andrews] Sisters said they made it a point to socialize with no one above the rank of sergeant—a bit of -democracy which cost them various kinds of special privileges, such as specially-assigned planes and private cars. Once, when invited to an officer's cocktail party, they turned down the invitation, declaring they hadn't come overseas to drink with officers."

The following letters represent some of the GI reaction to their interview:

Dear Editor:

I would like to make a complaint about all the baloney these camp show entertainers are giving out with when they get back to the States.

I am not a Special Service officer who is trying to cover some mistakes he or anyone else could have made in arranging the shows (for Mr. Jack Benny's information, they are not directors or producers, but Army men with a job to do), but I am a pilot and have flown these entertainers around in Europe and Africa on several occasions.

The Andrews Sisters made it a point to socialize with no one above the rank of sergeant, which cost them "special privileges" such as special assigned planes and private cars. I was at the airfield when they were flown in on a special plane. and I know the two pilots of that airplane very well. I was also standing there when they drove off in a *private* staff car. and I was at the table next to theirs at the officers' club when they were having cocktails with two lieutenant colonels and other high ranking officers.

I personally don't give a damn what special privileges they or anyone else gets, but it browns me off when they get back to the States and give with all this malarkey about all the undemocratic privileges the officers get.

—A Browned-Off Lieutenant

. . . I personally know of two nights, and I can name the dates, that the Andrews Sisters were guests of Army personnel above the grade of sergeant.

To my knowledge, no remarks have been made among enlisted personnel about the amount of time they spent with officers. They have given them the benefit of every doubt, because everyone knows it is very hard to distinguish between a lieutenant colonel and a sergeant.

—GI Joe

. . . I will admit the Andrews Sisters had a good show, and I believe everyone thoroughly enjoyed their act, but how can Maxene make a statement about not socializing with anyone above the rank of sergeant? I would just like to know since when have they started letting enlisted men in the ATC Officers' Club in Naples.

— Pfc. Wm. Reed, ATC

. . . If the Andrews Sisters maintain that they made it a point to socialize with no one above the rank of sergeant, then the two colonels and two captains they were with at the ATC Officers' Club in Naples on Aug. 8 must have been temporarily degraded by them to sergeant or below.

—Lt. David Kolodny, ATC

. . . The Andrews Sisters put on one of the best shows that I have seen, but when they said they did not socialize with anyone above the rank of sergeant, ask them what they were doing at the ATC Officers' Club in Naples. Is that a place where EM congregate?

—Cpl., ATC

CHAPTER 8
Civilian Life

BACK HOME MY IMMEDIATE PROBLEM was adjustments that had to be made after being elsewhere for four years. Overworked dry cleaning establishments who also did alterations were swamped. It seems that the returnees had taken on different dimensions in the interim and the old civilian clothes that they had left behind didn't come up to their new measurements.

Showing up for work was the next order of business, and we were greeted warmly almost all the way around. Another returnee, Ray Allemang, and I strolled into the Midway hangar and ran into veteran mechanic Manley, who was as good as they came—and as sarcastic or more so as they come. He greeted us and when I asked him, "You didn't expect us to come back, did you?" He answered, "I knew you'd come back; they don't make any Nazis smart enough to shoot you guys down."

There were some wrinkles, however, and a few of the pilots who had moved up to captain during our absence made it clear that since they had held down our jobs while we were gone, they should be able to keep them in a status quo situation. This idea ran up against a snag when one of these pilots informed Brigadier General Dick Petty of this fact. General Petty had also just returned from the war and was also vice president of Operations before and after the conflict. We never knew how that conversation turned out.

It seems that returning veterans were inclined to talk about their war experiences and to regale the folks with their adventures. This was boring to some listeners, and I heard a comment that was becoming standard: "It sure was a long war, wasn't it?" It was followed by an equally standard reply: "It sure was."

To shed the military discipline and customs took some effort. On one occasion I was waiting in the cockpit ready to start the engines when I noticed a cargo handler dragging his feet while loading a box aboard our plane. I called out the window, "Snap it up, will you?" He laid down the box, looked up at me and said, "You fly them and I'll load them." I got the picture.

On one DC-3 trip west out of Des Moines, Iowa, to Omaha, one of our lady passengers sent word up to the cockpit that she wished to tip the pilots twenty-five cents because she had been told that this was the thing to do. She didn't specify how the two-bits were to be divided, but I assumed that it would be fifteen cents for the captain and ten cents for the co-pilot. I went back to the cabin to return her gratuity, explaining that tipping wasn't allowed on airlines but that her offer was greatly appreciated. During our conversation it was revealed that she was born and raised on a small farm in northern Iowa, and on this very day she had taken her first automobile ride and, of course, was making her first airplane flight. Happenings like this almost made me feel like a pioneer.

On a trip out of Chicago scheduled to fly non-stop to Denver, one of our stewardesses came up to the cockpit and said that a soldier aboard had just pulled out a gun and taken a shot at her, the bullet grazing her leg and entering a stack of timetables. This called for an investigation, and as I was about to go back to the cabin, the second stewardess came up and handed me the gun, the timetables and the spent bullet. I went back to the cabin and the soldier stopped me and said, "Captain, I'd like to talk to you," and I indicated that I wanted to talk to him also. He said "These girls accused me of taking a shot at them, but you know how girls are."

Of course this guy had to be dumped; Omaha was just ahead, so that was where we were heading for an unscheduled stop. We requested that the local police and the military police meet us on our landing.

On landing, the M.P.s met us and said that they would take over from there. That was the end of this episode, except that our position reports after leaving Omaha drew comments over the air all night long from other trips around and listening. Every position report was greeted with such sterling gems as "bang, bang, bang." There appears to be no speedier communication system than that of an airline.

Returning to Chicago at 3:00 A.M. from an overnight trip from Newark to Allentown to Cleveland to Toledo, I tried to start my Model-A Ford in the parking lot. The wind was from the northwest at fifty-five miles per hour and the temperature was well below zero. Lifting the hood of my car in the parking lot I found a piece of the engine head about the size of a pie plate had lifted up about an inch, including a spark plug and one of the head bolts. This was similar to a frozen milk bottle with the cap pushed upward.

It was then that I had decided that there must be a better way to get along with nature, so we decided to move west to some-place like Denver, Colorado, for starters. And so we moved.

WHILE trying to sell our house in Western Springs, my wife and daughter remained behind and I started working out of Denver. I rented an upstairs room at a friend's house and waited for my family to join me. One Sunday morning after the night before, I was walking along the street to catch a bus to get some breakfast when I saw a bear perched up in a tree growling at me. I hurried along and got my breakfast and returned to my room to relate the bear encounter to my landlord. Things went from bad to worse, but the next morning I was vindicated when the local newspaper reported that a young bear had escaped from the zoo and ended up in a tree, where the zoo people coaxed him down with some honey spread around the tree. He was captured and returned to his rightful home.

My daughter attended high school during this period, and among her friends was a Persian girl who had just immigrated to this country. She spoke six different languages fluently, including English. We showed her around Colorado, and on one trip to the south, while expounding on the area I mentioned that there were still some wild buffalo roaming around. Just as I pointed, a huge bull buffalo made his way through the trees. He sure surprised me, for I had been handing out a bunch of Chamber of Commerce advertising with tongue in cheek, and little did I think that any of it was true.

Later I did a little bragging to the Persian lass and told her that I had almost met Joe Stalin. The "almost" part was a special mission flight during WWII that I had drawn. This flight was to take Ambassador Davies on a 'round-the-world junket via Moscow. We had a C-87 converted into a luxury plane with sleeping quarters, a galley and other VIP trimmings. My crew had been ordered to get special new uniforms, since we were to meet Stalin in Moscow. Special food was to be put aboard and the ambassador's personal chef was to be part of the crew. I was taken to the secret weather service in Washington and briefed on the expected weather conditions for this 'round-the-world trip.

Since the trip was to proceed from Moscow through Siberia, touching down at Irkutz and Yakutz, the cold capital of the world, en route to Alaska and back to Washington, the airports along the way were mostly unknown to the Air Corps. I had been given a camera to bring back some snapshots of the landing fields, but I was cautioned that if the camera were confiscated, it would be my own personal camera and not that of the U.S. Government.

The aircraft, the crew and the special foods had all been assembled at Washington National Airport for the trip that never was—at least not for me. Mr. Davies showed up with his entourage, our crew and all emergency equipment was in place, and the trip was ready to be launched. The plane was being fueled to capacity when the fuel cells sprang a leak and gasoline flowed all over the tarmac. The plane had been prepared to the fullest extent for this mission, except that the fuel tanks had not been filled to capacity.

The equipment and the cabin personnel were hastily transferred to a DC-4 to be flown by a commercial crew, and my dream trip had become just that. Mr. Davies asked me why I wasn't flying the mission, but the only explanation was that higher-ups had decided in favor of a commercial crew.

After this lengthy narrative of my "almost" trip, the Persian girl quietly said, "I knew Mr. Stalin; he had a shriveled-up arm." I wish these kids would stop putting me down.

BUT Denver didn't measure up to our expectations, especially in the fishing department. After two years trying for the gamy ones with little to show, heading west seemed to be the best move. That we did, moving to Palos Verdes Estates in California.

At this new base I was just another seniority number, which meant that the younger hopefuls who were waiting in the wings for the prime spots were not pleased to have Easterners move in and set them back. At my first pilots meeting with management, the superintendent of flying said to me, "Welcome to Los Angeles from all of the pilots who are senior to you," and that's the way it turned out.

In Los Angeles several charters were thrown my way, one of which was a movie charter in a DC-6 to Farmington, New Mexico. We were to pick up a movie group on location in Farmington. I was given the takeoff weights, information on the field and a special caution that there was a new asphalt apron in front of the terminal and, since it was rather thin and wouldn't support a machine as heavy as the one we were using, the station manager requested that we stay clear of this macadam mat. Also, a Frontier airliner was to meet our flight with a special loading stand which was not available at this field.

Arriving over the airport, I felt a sense of being alone in a far-off place with no Big-Daddy looking over my shoulder. I had an empty plane and a nice group of people waiting for our arrival, so I decided to zoom low over the field to observe closely the lay of the land. This was to be the first large four-engine aircraft to land at this drome.

After zooming around to look over the terrain, we landed and the Frontier airliner landed immediately afterward with the loading stand.

As we approached the loading area, the lead man appeared and waved us in with authentic style. He brought me right down the middle of the off-limits tarmac. At the sign of the engine cut-off I glanced to my right to see another man jumping up and down and tearing his hair out. This was the real station manager; my pseudo-lead man—imitating the real thing, and doing it very well. His name was Rory Calhoun, the star of the movie *Girls of the Golden West.*

The first person to meet us after these aerial didoes was an inspector from the CAA who had watched all of this arrival. He disappeared and wasn't around at our departure. This takeoff was spectacular, for the runway was rough, up hill and dale with a bend in the middle. After leaving the ground we dipped low behind the hills and went on our way.

We kept the cockpit door open since this was a private charter, and some of the passengers came up to look around. One of those on board was an Indian chief who was well known in movie circles. He looked around and grunted, "Huh, flying southwest, eh?"

ONE afternoon in Palos Verdes I received a call from Atlantic Richfield Oil Company, which was sponsoring a daily news program. At that time my daughter was working for the company as a paleontologist. They had just received a news bulletin that sixteen people were reported missing on a rafting trip down the Colorado River and that one of the missing persons was my daughter.

A lifetime of flashes shot through my mind: Were they drowned? Did some of them make it to the banks of the river, and other possibilities. After a few stunned minutes I mustered forces and went into action. My alma mater, the Air Corps, would be contacted immediately, so I called the U.S. Air Force base in Phoenix, Arizona, since that was the closest one in the area. The officer of the day listened to my story and told me that he would check with the base in Salt Lake to verify my story and would call me back shortly.

I leaped to the phone when it rang, and it was the officer of the day keeping his promise. Salt Lake had confirmed my tale of woe and the base was organized and readied to go ahead with the rescue operation. A refueling tanker was readied and a number of aircraft and their crews were standing by. I owe a lot to the U.S. Air Corps, but this is my biggest I.O.U.

Next in line in my rescue plan was contacting UAL, my employer. Calling dispatch, I requested that the pilot of the overnight flight to Chicago try to observe any kind of activity in the area, even if it might be only the flicker of a flashlight or a camping lantern.

Exhausted, I sat around and waited for any news, good, bad or indifferent. About midnight, the phone rang and my daughter, in person, asked me, "Dad, have you heard anything on the radio about anything?" Then I got the whole story. It seemed that on a run down the rapids two of the occupants had been thrown overboard and decided that they had had enough of the trip and were beached. They wrote a message on the sand that said "help." A small plane from nearby had seen the message, and had started the entire scenario.

THE first pressurized airline, the DC-6, showed up, and we went to San Francisco for our checkout. About this time my wife decided to become a medical doctor and made plans to attend the Women's Medical College in Philadelphia. This decision took about five years, during which my personal life became somewhat askew. Being a married man without a wife put quite a dent in my modest social life. It seems like the best deals come in pairs, so I lost out.

With so much extra time on my hands I joined the Sierra Club on a junket to South America. I planned to join the group at Lima, Peru, after a visit to the pre-Inca ruins at Machu Picchu on my own. On the way over to Cuzco, the start of the auto-rail to the ruins, I identified myself to the crew as an airline pilot and was invited to ride in the cockpit as far as Cuzco. The crew was most cordial and mentioned that the brakes on the Constellation had failed on the inbound trip and they were hoping that they would hold during the landing in Cuzco, which was 10,000 feet above sea level, and a mite short to boot.

We flew at 20,000 feet in and around many spectacular peaks in the Andes with myself a little concerned about the performance of the brakes and how they would do on the landing.

We arrived in good shape and I repaired to the only hotel in Cuzco for some much-needed rest. But when I arrived at the hotel without a reservation, I was told that the place was full, but if necessary they would let me sleep on the clay floor of the basement which was a storage place for mattresses and other hotel equipment.

At this altitude I began to get a good case of altitude sickness, and even a clay floor sounded good to me. No sooner had I conked out than the hotel manager awakened me and said, "I can't let you sleep down here; you are from our sister city of Santa Barbara, so come with me." He had mysteriously managed to find a luxurious suite that was still available, and I was moved from the basement to the top bracket of quarters. At this point it didn't make any difference to me whether I slept on a dirt floor or a king-size water bed.

The trip to the ruins at Machu Picchu on the auto-rail and the mini bus to the top was a fine experience with a lot of 3-D photo opportunities as long as you clicked your camera before noon, when the clouds usually moved in. But the Sierra Club was waiting for me to join them at Lima, so I returned via the same route and made the connection.

This Sierra Club group consisted of thirty members and about eight cooks and other helpers to make our trip comfortable. We were supposedly prepared not only to camp out in earthy conditions and others along the way, but also equipped to visit with civic officials and others of importance during the trip. A reception by the mayor of Valparaiso, Chile, brought us in with hiking boots and other camping garb.

In preparing for this trip I assumed that the club was an experienced outing group that would show up with all of the necessary equipment and supplies for a close look at nature's adventures. In order to keep up with the group I brought along such items as a roll of toilet paper, a can of peanuts, a bottle of bourbon and a plastic fold-up tent.

One of the first overnight stays was at the Chilean Army's ski troop training headquarters, where we Sierra Club folks were to be hosted. The military personnel were anxiously waiting for our arrival and instead of being a bunch of young athletic types we showed up with a mixture of such folks as a seventy-year-old miner's wife, a geologist and his wife, a Peace Corpsman, several mountain climbers, two fishermen, including myself, and the other fisherman's wife, who was a bird watcher—a real collection of real people.

The military had prepared a bunch of crab burgers for our arrival, but since we arrived three hours late, the burgers were sitting in the hot sun, over-ripening and getting worse. Most of our bunch were famished by the time we arrived, and waded into the burgers with gusto. I did my best to tell them that they shouldn't appease their appetites with these well-intentioned offerings which had been deteriorating in the sun for hours, but they didn't listen; they were just plain hungry.

This army building was only designed for men, so when we showed up with a mixture of both men and women—and a troubled mixture at that—things began to happen. The crab burger thing sent many of our group down the proverbial drain. It didn't seem to matter what sex you were; the stool was the order of the day. The stools were all in a line and wide open, with no privacy whatsoever. Although I was one of the few who had no problem, I did have occasion to sit next to one of our ladies who was in trouble and who seemed to care less about the male next door.

Soon the group found out that I had the only roll of toilet paper aboard and sized me up as an inconsiderate clod when I didn't volunteer to share it with them. But what was one roll of toilet paper among thirty folks who were enjoying the Incan revenge, especially since it belonged to the only one not afflicted?

Camps along the way included a monastery up in the Andes, the Patagonia jungle and Puerta Monte on the southern tip of South America. Our food along the way was reasonably good and was occasionally augmented by a catch of fresh fish caught by Jack Welch and myself, the two fishermen in the group. I latched on to a twenty-pound land-locked salmon which was later poached to perfection for our club. A standing ovation was my reward when the group ate all of the salmon down to the ribs.

The camp at the monastery up in the Andes near the "Christ of the Andes" at 14,000 feet above sea level was cold and windy. Here the mountain climbers of our group took off to tackle a high peak. They had to quit halfway because of a blizzard. I prefer more comfortable activities and instead visited a huge copper mine that was run by an American. He jeeped me through long tunnels to view the operation, which was more to my liking, altitude-wise. I asked him about the possibility of uranium being there, but he said, "Forget it."

The finest camp of all was in Patagonia, where we occupied a beautiful valley amid icy streams and waterfalls from the surrounding glaciers. I made my first cast into a likely looking stream and the water boiled with activity. This was trout fishing at its best, and our camp finally began to get their fill of fish.

On the return home we stopped over in Panama and were invited to boat over to the Smithsonian Institute's research facility on the island of Barro Colorado in Lake Gatun on the Panama Canal. This island was isolated from civilization and inhabited by numerous wild animals and interesting flora. We were permitted to roam the jungle and to observe the research projects. The woods were full of many species of monkeys, beautiful birds, coral snakes and javelina, one of which appeared out of the woods, unafraid of us humans, and nibbled on my Hush Puppies. Later I inquired of the Hush Puppy makers why this wild boar had taken a liking to my shoes. Their reply was that he recognized a relative. As a reward, I got a Hush Puppy shoe polishing kit.

*

SINCE I was to be without a wife for a few years, I decided to make good use of my spare time by becoming rich by any means available at the time. In those days, however, there was no lottery, no TV evangelist route and not even Las Vegas as a way to get rich. Had I had a choice, I might have selected the TV evangelist thing where you have the best of both worlds. Tax-free estates from here to there, unlimited expense accounts and even girls, if you will. What more could a man want?

Instead, I selected the uranium rush of the 1950s as my path to riches. I was to become a big, fat millionaire; not that I was fat—that would come later.

So I started out by enlisting the help of my neighbor friend, Bob Noble, and we bought a beat-up Jeep and a $500 scintalometer, camping gear, a bottle of Jack Daniels desert dew—which was only to be used in case of emergency, which was most of the time—and some dynamite for prospecting purposes.

The dynamite thing was exciting to Bob and me, if not to Red Adair, the legendary oil-well fire fighter. We made our first purchase of these sticks in Riverside, California. Before we were given the stuff, we had to get some details on how not to blow ourselves up. First the demonstrator bounced a stick on the counter and said, "See, it won't go off." In a few minutes, Bob and I came back into the store and bought the dynamite. On our way out we were given a parting warning: don't keep the percussion caps anywhere near the dynamite.

Out in the desert near Twenty-nine Palms, after a few nervous blasts it got to be fun and we began to think of ourselves as "pros." We found one hot spot which looked promising and a claim was filed. Desert tortoises were plentiful then, but are now just about extinct, and the claim became the "Tortoise." The spot was rich in copper and went off the scale of the scintalometer, mostly around a huge boulder about twelve feet high.

It seemed to Bob and me that this mammoth boulder must be sitting on top of the main go, so we hammered and chiseled away for hours without changing the shape or size of this lid on our new fortune, so it had to be removed. We packed all of the remaining dynamite into one lump and placed it under the boulder. To this potential carnage we attached plenty of fuse, which we lit and ran like mad.

Later, we learned that the blast was heard as far away as the Marine base in Twenty-nine Palms, and we could see boulders rolling down the hills around us. After the blast Bob reached the scene first, and I found him sitting on a rock, laughing himself sick. There was no trace of the boulder and no more radiation was found. We had blown away our entire fortune and the Tortoise turned out to be nothing more than a piece of ground with a dent in it.

There must be a better way to get rich, I reasoned, so I tried another approach. A bracket was rigged to hold the scintalometer on a rented Cessna 170, and I began prospecting from the air. This horsing around the canyons and over the desert in a small plane provided more adventures in a day than a year of airline flying.

To rent this little hissing monster I had to check out in it first. The check pilot was a jovial, red headed pilot, who was also a girl. Her first admonishment was, "I want your to watch out for those airline pilots; they'll run right over you." Up to that time I hadn't known that we airline pilots were held in such high esteem by the small-plane fraternity.

My checkout ride took us over the city of Los Angeles, and the girl had brought along a sack of apples which she munched during the test. The cores were thrown out of the window, and Johnny Appleseed did all right with his apple seeds, so perhaps Los Angeles might become the apple center of the world.

The rented Cessna was based at Hawthorne airport, which was a short landing strip just east of Los Angeles International Airport. Returning from a prospecting trip one day, I called the Hawthorne tower and without thinking I said, "Hawthorne tower, this is United 56 Charlie. I'm ten miles east and request landing instructions."

There was a loud noise like someone falling off of a stool and a bunch of clicking sounds. Then a voice, short of breath, came on with, "Are you landing here, United?" I corrected my mistake, but it must have been a telling experience for this tower man.

Years later a United flight piloted by a takeover Pan Am pilot tried to land at this same tiny airstrip at night, but discovered his mistake in time and proceeded to the main go at LAX. When I heard this I sincerely hoped that the same tower operator hadn't been on duty when I made my request. The man would be on the verge of a nervous breakdown.

Using the flying scintalometer I located several hot spots from the air, but when I visited them with my Jeep I found that they had already been taken. Not only that, one of the spots, after weeks of mining, produced a mere $1300 worth of uranium, but at a cost of $1200. I soon realized that this was obviously not the best way to make a bundle.

Being a 3-D photographer, I needed some photos of the actual mining itself. I visited a working mine near Beatty, Nevada, with the idea of investing in a good prospect and sampling the ore, and also getting a few good 3-D pictures.

I ate the miner's stew, worked alongside the miners and entered the mine tunnel to get my pictures. The din from the jackhammer was deafening and the tunnel was fogged by haze. As I approached the apparent spot where the miner was working with his miner's lamp, I set off my flash. I was only a few feet away from his eyes, which must have been dilated in the darkness, and he was blinded. The jack-hammer stopped and he shouted, "What the hell?" I ran back through the tunnel, barking my elbows along the way, and made my escape. This was the finale on my road to riches.

I RETAINED my commission in the Air Corps with some two-week active-duty assignments on an M-Day basis until the beginning of the Korean War conflict, after which I elected to give up my pay status and return to inactive status. I felt that one war

was enough and, financially, my civilian job was more rewarding.

One of my active duty assignments was to Fairfield-Suison
Travis AFB in Northern California. Reporting in to the C.O., I
announced that I desired some choice cross-country trips including a reconn flight over the north pole on my tour where I could
look at the Russians eye to eye as we passed each other over the
top of the world.

He replied with authority that things had changed in the Air
Corps since I had last served. Pointing to a desk in the far corner,
he added that it would be mine for the two weeks. Elaborating
further, he outlined my new duties, which would include training
in such fascinating subjects as procurement, cost-effective operations and other financial aspects of the new Air Corps. Up to this
point my main interest in such matters had consisted of little
more than trying to balance my personal checkbook.

However, a couple of interesting missions alleviated the initial
shock, and the tour ended up satisfactorily. The flight over the
north pole required a security check which could not have been
completed within the two-week period, so that idea was
scrubbed.

Instead I was assigned to a weather observation flight as one
of three pilots in the crew of a seventeen-hour mission out over
the Pacific to a point well beyond Honolulu and a return to
Travis. This was in pre-satellite days, and this banana run determined such weather factors as temperatures, dew points, precipi-
tation and atmospheric pressure.

All night long at frequent intervals on the outbound leg, the
B-29 was depressurized and the exact altitude above the ocean,
as determined by the radar altimeter, maintained at which the
readings were recorded. The process was repeated on the return
leg except that the altitude was 30,000 feet above sea level. Sev-
enteen hours aloft is a long time, so the flying was divided
among the three pilots with rest periods back in the cabin on top
of life rafts and parachutes. Enough fatigue can make these
bunks quite comfortable enough. At the end of the flight at 3:00

the following afternoon I was already making plans to head for the nearest bunk for recovery, but much to my surprise the young, bushy-tailed Air Corps captain in charge decided that he would do a simulated instrument approach to Travis. So much for callow youth; personally I was in favor of getting this noisy beast back on the ground as soon as possible.

Still another mission to which I was assigned aided in relieving the strain and tension of my desk job. This was a DC-4 flight to Anchorage, Alaska, and on to Shemya, an island in the chain very close to Siberia. This crew consisted of two Air Corps pilots and myself, the airline member who was on two weeks' active duty as a reserve officer.

On this round trip I drew the leg from Anchorage to Shemya on the outer chain. The weather on our arrival was heavy rain, low fog and a strong crosswind for the landing runway. The radar approach was known as a ground-controlled approach, and was something we did not yet have on the airline, so this was my first attempt. I followed the controller's instructions to the letter, and when we broke out of the clouds just a few feet off the ocean I saw nothing but an angry ocean and no place to go. The strong wind across the runway caused us to crab to the left for compensation, and I got my first view of the runway by looking out of the copilot's window. After we landed, the controller who brought me in called and complimented me on my performance and I returned the compliment, since he had taken us right down the centerline without any directional changes in the process. Little did he know that I had only done exactly what he had told me to do.

YOU'D THINK REGINALD WOULD AT
LEAST WAIT UNTIL HE GT HIS UNIFORM OFF

"STINKY" VON RECTANGLE

YACHTSMAN
VON RECTANGLE

*A few drawings showing
what some of my crews
thought about me. Others
will not be mentioned here.*

Pilots think radar is one of the greatest advances in airline history. Here's what United Captain C. E. Recknagel says about it:

Smoother flights on United . . . the only coast-to-coast airline with RADAR on every plane

"For you, the passenger, radar means smoother rides and more on-time arrivals. That's because radar scans the sky up to 150 miles ahead—showing the pilot the smoothest course in any weather. And now, on United, you can be certain of this extra comfort and dependability because every United plane is equipped with radar."

FLY UNITED — WORLD'S LARGEST RADAR FLEET

CHAPTER 9

The Jet Age

I MOVED UP THE LADDER TO THE DC-7s and Boeing Stratocruisers and entered the jet age, something new and different from any previous step in airline progress. The Air Corps already had these new machines in operation and had encountered some new aspects of sub-sonic flying. One of these foibles was that aborting a takeoff when a mechanical failure reared it's ugly head usually resulted in a heap at the end of the runway. It seemed that the desk engineers could have been wrong in their calculations on stopping distances when a failure happened during takeoff.

Another surprise was the "coffin corner" situation, a new altitude and airspeed phenomenon that the Wright Brothers hadn't contemplated. At a specific altitude for each aircraft type things begin to happen when the stall speed, the overspeed and the jet engine fuel controller all take over at the same time. In other words there is no option for the pilot who can either cut the power to slow down and stall out or increase the power and do a high speed stall out—both bum choices.

I had gotten wind of these things, and since I had been appointed chairman of the ALPA Safety Committee, Fifth Region, and an associate member of the CAA, Fourth Region, and since there was a safety meeting coming up for all of the airline pilots in the Los Angeles area, I thought it might be a good idea to invite a speaker who was a proven expert in the field. My choice was Chuck Yeager, who was then a major and the first test pilot to survive while breaking through the sound barrier.

Yeager landed at the Los Angeles airport in a small AT-6 trainer exactly on time, and my wife and I drove him to the meeting hall where he gave a fine talk on the the future of the jet world.

The aircraft simulator for any airplane type is one of the most valuable pieces of machinery for actually training a pilot in all phases of his profession without damage to an airplane or anything else except his ego. Pretense calls for the trainee to actually fly a plane, with the plane acting accordingly, but the combination is on the ground. All sorts of emergencies can be inserted into the system without the loss of aircraft or human lives.

As in any other system, comics have their say. The screen portrays a view of the runway and surroundings on an approach under favorable weather conditions, but it is actually a large wall in a nearby hangar, and the simulator bug portrays this scene.

On one of my simulated checkouts in the DC-6 I had survived a lot of input emergencies and was supposedly cruising along at 21,000 feet above sea level and waiting for the next emergency, when the side window of the windshield opened and a flight manager stuck his head in and said "Hi." This meant that I was flying at 21,000 feet, but some guy opened the window and said "Hi."

Another wit pulled up a toy truck across the runway just as the pilot was about to land. This was fun for the participants, but not so pleasurable for the victims.

Approaching the jet age, management seemed to be more concerned with our entry and potential safety problems than the pilots, who were looking forward to the transition. The most difficult part of the checkout was management's excessive concern, as well as that of the FAA personnel, who were also treading new turf. This apparently spilled over to a few of the pilots and might have had some influence on the ones who did not make the checkout on their first attempt.

My own rating ride could have been an example of this pressure. Our UAL Flight Standards Captain Park Learned was co-pilot, and the FAA inspector sat in the observer's seat giving the orders. One maneuver was to completely stall the plane until it actually started to spin, and then make the recovery. Our UAL man objected strenuously to this, since a few days before another DC-8 had been out doing the same maneuvers, and had developed many leaks in the wing fuel tanks and drooled kerosene all over the Denver ramp. The FAA man and our check pilot got into a heated discussion about policy while I cringed in the middle with my checkout hanging in the balance. Captain Learned stood his ground on this one, but it took a long time and I was finally allowed to bring the plane up only to stick-shaker speed before recovery. The stick shaker is a warning device that shakes the control column violently just before a complete stall.

Then we went to the low circling approach over a nearby auxiliary field which would be used when landing under low-cloud conditions. I did this maneuver successfully, but another argument started up with our UAL pilot approving my performance and the FAA man stating that he didn't like to see any pilot circling so abruptly that close to the ground. But I made it through that one and we came to the final test, which was an instrument approach to the Denver airport with myself under a hood that prevented me from seeing anything outside of the plane, but only the instruments inside the cockpit. All through the approach the FAA man kept poking his head in front of my face and watching my eyes. I didn't know what he was looking for, but I do know that he saw a pair of eyeballs darting about and scanning the many instruments on the control panel. Just before landing another monkey wrench was thrown into the works. The instrument landing system had become inoperative and it was necessary to circle and land on a smaller runway. Another UAL flight manager called from the ground and directed that only a rated pilot would be allowed to land on this runway. The FAA man was then on the spot. Obviously he wanted to give me the usual lecture about flying after we were on the ground and before he granted me my license. He growled at this turn of events but said that I could make the landing, thereby acknowledging that I had passed the test and was now a DC-8 jet pilot.

But once on the ground he still gave me a stern lecture about circling at low altitude, although he admitted that I had been in full control of the airplane and that he had confidence in my ability to fly the jets. Little did he know that I had been raised in low altitude flying back in Galveston and not only by myself, but sometimes in tight formations of groups of three up to six hundred planes, all JUST OFF THE GROUND.

Many years later I would have liked to have him aboard on my approach to the airport in Seoul, Korea, when we circled close to the ground, not only because of the fog but also because of the requirement that we fly low over the field and circle before landing for identification purposes.

The coast-to-coast jet run generated a civic problem at Kennedy Airport— namely jet noise. The neighbors around the airport began making more noise than our jets. It's true that a departing jet creates a lot of racket, so in order to appease the complainers numerous tricky procedures were developed, such as exceptionally steep climb-outs, sharp turns right after takeoffs and other schemes which would ordinarily be classed as danger-ous maneuvers. A steep climb departure calls for gaining as much altitude as quickly as possible, even at the cost of some air-speed to cover a loss of power or other contingencies, and could result in some loss of control over the aircraft.

It was not too surprising then when an American Airlines pi-lot, while complying with this noise abatement program, went in as he made his turn just off the ground, with the loss of everyone aboard. Had he had a little more airspeed or some additional al-titude he could have saved the day by being able to overcome the electrical control problem without strain.

The noise problem at Kennedy became so serious that a sound truck was placed at the end of the runway, and each de-parting aircraft was given a decibel rating that was forwarded to the airline involved.

There might have been a bit of competition between the San Francisco and Los Angeles pilots as to who could generate the most decibels, and I might have been among the leaders. On my way into the office of the boss to explain my way out of my sev-enth violation, I found still another notice in my mailbox to the effect that I had yet another violation to my credit. So I explained to him that I took off, saw the ground truck, and everything went black. I just dove right down on the S.O.B.

After shuttling around the domestic routes it became time to move up to the posh Hawaiian run, which required certain ditching training for the crews. One requirement was the ability to swim the length of an Olympic-size swimming pool. Being the poor swimmer that I am, this requirement forced me to take numerous swimming lessons at the YMCA in both San Pedro and later in Santa Barbara.

At the San Pedro YMCA we could drop in at any time, shower and enter the pool without the hindrance of swim shorts, since only males were involved. On one such visit I entered the pool area and saw another man clinging to the edge of the pool and shaking his head, giving me some kind of signal that all was not well. Then I looked toward the other end of the pool and saw the reason for his concern. The secretary of the Y had just brought in two of her friends to show them around the establishment. I sure spoiled a good thing, because shortly afterward trunks were mandatory.

Later, while training in Santa Barbara, a well-known movie personage usually joined me around noon for a refreshing dip in the dew. He would come out of the shower room roaring like a bull and beating his chest before plunging into the pool with one gigantic splash. One day I mentioned to him that this was sure better than drinking a few martinis at noon, whereupon he replied, "I don't know about that, I always have a couple before coming over here."

The final swim test was held in San Francisco and went well for me, but surprisingly enough one Hawaiian prospective cabin attendant was unable to swim the distance. I was under the impression that all Hawaiians were as good under the water as above. But I passed the test and got a handshake from the guy in charge.

In the pool a twenty-five-man life raft was inflated and we had to climb aboard, which was not an easy task since the sides were three feet high. For these tests several applicants had to borrow swimsuits. One of the men borrowed a suit that was much too large for him and they slipped off when he made his dive into the water. Another borrowed suit for one of the girls was also too big, which created a serious distraction for some of us.

Further tests took place aboard a discarded DC-7, the last of the propeller driven airliners, which was anchored out in San Francisco Bay for this purpose. A complete ditching was simulated, including radio May Day signals and boarding the 25-man life raft.

Then came the sun canopy, the shark repellent, the signal flare and the Gibson Girl, which was an emergency self-propelled radio transmitter. Later the DC-7 was removed from San Francisco Bay because of the adverse effect on passengers departing from the airport and looking down on what appeared to be a crashed plane.

All of this training seemed appropriate at the time but many questions surfaced during this period. Assuming a successful landing at sea, would hundreds of passengers be able to survive as though they were all well-trained Marines able to carry out orders to the letter? The passenger list might consist of some elderly, babes in arms and others of lesser physical ability. The training served it's purpose then, but is of less importance in the modern jet age.

Another step before flying west was to familiarize myself with the islands, their history, airports and anything else that might be useful to a pilot flying this run. This was the easiest and most enjoyable requirement of all when the Flight Manager Captain Ed Kiessig, with a twinkle in his eye, instructed me to get familiar with everything about the islands, right down to where the pineapples were grown— or at least where they could be found. For this task I was given unlimited access to the cockpits of Hawaiian Airlines on their routes around the islands and told to do my thing.

The pilots and station managers of the airline went overboard to assist me, and any flight to whichever island seemed to be flown for my benefit. Sometimes we flew low along the cliffs of Molokai to look at the many waterfalls and get a close look at the leper colony on the point. At Lanai, the pineapple island, the crew showed me where they got their pineapples, whereupon the copilot stepped off the plane, gathered a few along the runway, and on we went with the passengers aboard.

At Maui I was greeted by the station manager, who overwhelmed me with attention worthy of someone of importance, not an airline captain who was just looking over the terrain to see what was what. I visited a pineapple processing plant and then a macadamia nut cannery. By this time I had built up a lot of excess baggage, such as boxes of pineapples and cases of macadamia nuts, and was tired of lugging the stuff around, so I tried to cut off any future gifts.

Kona, on the west coast of the big island, was a rewarding stop where I met Walter Peirrara, the station manager, and his wife after which we became friends for many years. I even brought a teddy bear for their newborn son, but some Christmas cards later Walter sent me a depressing card saying that his boy had been killed in a car accident over the hump from Hilo to Kona.

On this first visit to Kona I caught a modest-size marlin that weighed in at 185 pounds. They were having a lean season here at the time and were looking for some kind of boost in the tourist trade. My modest catch almost made me a celebrity, and on the return to Honolulu the crew made note of my catch and the radio and news media made mention of the event. My exciting catch seemed impressive to me, but somewhat trivial when compared to the 1,300-pounder previously snagged.

At Hana, on the eastern side of Maui, I requested that the crew stick around until I could find out whether I had a place to stay for the night. Some time before, in Honolulu, I had met a man and his wife and son strolling around the streets of Waikiki, and since they had seemed like a nice family I offered them a round of drinks, which were malted milks. As I stepped off the plane at Hana none other than the same man greeted me. He was now the manager of the Hana Plantation and I was assured that I most certainly had a place to bunk down. My bunk was to be the Marshall Field suite at the Plantation. I waved goodbye to the crew.

At this posh resort I rattled around by myself for several days, and when I checked out, the desk clerk told me that he could find no charges, so my bill was nothing—well, almost nothing; there was a tab for the round of malted milks rolled up sometime before in Waikiki.

And so I arrived at the pinnacle of runs, from Los Angeles to Honolulu. This deluxe operation had few weather problems and was certainly an enjoyable way to earn a living. Our layovers in Honolulu were at the old Moana, Princess Kauilani, Illakai or the Royal Hawaiian, where permanent rooms were maintained by United. Unlike the average traveler, who must dig up his own transportation and lodging, our crews always had a limousine waiting for them at the airport and a room at a posh hotel with nothing left but time for rest and recreation.

The layovers included many forms of recreation, which made for pleasant living. Some went surfing on a regular basis, others played bridge in the hotel lobby of the Moana, still others biked around or rented Jeeps for junkets into the interior of Oahu. Just plain bird watching was another popular activity. I indulged in most of these except for surfing and the playing of bridge.

An air traffic controller aboard a flight to the islands invited me and any other member of the crew to drop in for a tour of the traffic control facility located inside the crater at Diamond Head. A stewardess and I accepted the invitation and rented bikes to pedal out to Diamond Head. We showed up at the reception desk and requested to see our host, who would show us around.

When the controller showed up he appeared to be uncertain as to whether this was such a good idea after all. The stewardess was in shorts and favorably so, but he recovered nicely and showed us through as promised. Rows of controllers seemed entranced as we walked through, just as we were fascinated by the oceanic traffic system in operation. But the traffic flowed smoothly that day and everyone seemed happy.

I showed up at the Los Angeles airport parking lot for my outbound trip of the day when I met the inbound crew, which had just landed from Honolulu. They were laughing so hard they could barely tell me the reason for this bit of levity. But it finally came out that a passenger named Harry Richmond, the entertainer mentioned earlier, had gotten a very important member of his anatomy caught in his zipper while visiting the rest room. The pilot, Lennie Jones, radioed dispatch requesting medical help on their arrival at Los Angeles. The radio operator kept bugging Lenny as to the details of the medical problem. Lenny refrained from giving out any intimate details over the air as long as he could and then gave up, saying "He got it caught in his zipper."

This period of shuttling back and forth between the mainland and Honolulu was punctuated by an occasional fishing trip to Baja in Mexico. My second officer at the time was Bob Horne, who owned a four-place Mooney and I was invited on many trips to the peninsula. The adventures in Baja included little-bird landings at such spots as Loretta, Bahia de las Palmas, Mulege, Bahia de Los Angeles, Buena Vista and others. It was a good sport to navigate by the old tried and true method of timing your progress and estimating your arrival over the next point, and this is how we got around in Baja.

On one of these trips we arrived at a place called Amy's Ranch shortly before dark and without much petrol showing on the gauge because of headwinds. We landed just before pitch darkness on a small dirt strip near the ranch, but the storm that had just passed through had left a pond of water between our plane and the resort.

We had to get to the lodging some way or another so Bob and I decided to take off and land closer in. We did that, but while circling around in the black of night we couldn't find the strip, especially since there was not even a flicker of light on the ground to help us. After several tries we talked ourselves into a landing, out of fuel and out of breath.

It was really cold that night and since Amy told us that she had no gasoline available for us to continue our flight we would have to spend the night as her guests until the next day, when a plane would arrive with gasoline. Sure enough, the next day the B-23 arrived with the petrol and we were on our way. The B-23 was a WWII favorite of mine, a clone of the old DC-3 but much faster. I do believe that Amy had the gas already but needed some visitors to break up the monotony of this secluded spot. Amy was a retired New York stage actress who ran this spread in the Baja.

While flying to the islands I was offered a part-time job with a Santa Barbara research firm that had a one-year contract with the FAA to study the economic impact of weather on all phases of flying. The personnel who took part in this study were:

Gene Bollay, president of the research firm;

Walter Koch, for general aviation;

Professor M. Andron, for economics;

Captain Carl Recknagel, for air carriers;

John Cronin, for general research.

Many other agencies and qualified experts in their field also assisted in the research. Upon completion of the study the document was submitted to a representative of the FAA for approval. He picked up the final report and said he would take it to Las Vegas for five days for an in-depth study and would come back with any recommended changes or corrections. The report was approved and returned with a few minor changes penciled in— mostly in the format, but nothing about the contents, which speaks well of our efforts, I think.

MEANWHILE, my wife pursued her chosen career as a medical doctor and spent five years at the Women's Medical College in Philadelphia while I became a married man with a wife who wasn't there. Being married without a wife was a tad different from having one at your side. I rattled around feeling like neither fish nor fowl, but I survived.

She graduated from medical school, did her internship and

residency and became a pediatrician with a nice practice in Santa Barbara. I was nearing retirement and she was becoming somewhat financially independent, so for whatever reason I was served with divorce papers. The trial was a mean one that lasted for five full days in court, with myself coming out a limp and exhausted winner.

Being a newly minted single man at my age changed many things, and while waiting on the windup of the divorce trial I met a young lady, Mary Leppla, who was a divorcée and a realtor with two teenage kids. This was a mite different from being the spouse of a medical director with a good practice. I married her, and different it was.

VIET NAM brought United into the picture on a contract basis, with the Air Force to fly supplies and personnel to the Philippines and on to Viet Nam, Bangkok, Thailand and Seoul, Korea. I put in for this assignment about a year before my retirement, and it was a fortunate request because the mechanics went out on strike and all of United's operations were shut down except for the military flights to the Pacific. So I lucked out on that one and was employed right up to my retirement.

The routine during this final chapter of my flying career was to dead-head from Santa Barbara to San Francisco, where we picked up a DC-8 cargo-liner, ferrying it to Fairfield-Susan AFB, where it was loaded with supplies for the Pacific War theater. These excursions were interesting and not too difficult to fly. The weather consisted of some nasty thunderstorms around the Philippines and Saigon, plus a hurricane or two to spice up a flight. A weather-mapping radar device aboard the plane contributed much to the comfortable feeling through these areas.

On a departure from Clark AFB in the Philippines the briefing officer gave us the word about arriving at Tan San Nut, Saigon, airdome. Any civilian aircraft had to approach the field at 3000 feet to avoid small-arms fire from the Viet Cong surrounding the airport, then make a dive for the ground and the landing.

The departure was just as interesting, and we were warned

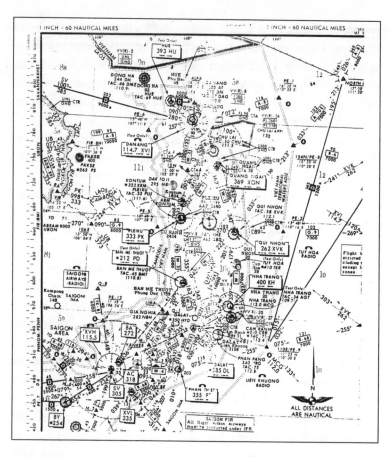

Aerial road map of the Saigon area.

that there would be a steady stream of helicopters flying across the runway and that they would always be below our flight path, especially if we climbed fast enough. On one of these departures, when I thought I was safely on my way, a four-plane flight of fighters flew through us from the rear. It was not too tight a formation because the leader went overhead and his three crewmen scraped underneath.

The arrival at Seoul, Korea, was almost as interesting because the briefing officer at Clark Field told us that we would not land right off the bat but would cruise down the runway at low altitude for identification purposes, then circle and land. Our arrival was at just about the same time that the fog lifted a bit and the circling was just off the ground, which is my bag.

Usually this maneuver would be considered a "no-no" for civilian operations, so it was a pleasure to get off the legal path occasionally and do it like in the good old days. The FAA inspector who awarded me my right to fly a DC-8 jet would have denied me the jet rating had I tried such a maneuver.

Going down for breakfast one morning in Santa Barbara, a young man stopped me and said, "You look okay to me. I'm a Marine with the First Division and I'm here on two weeks R&R from Viet Nam." His face was a bit beaten up and he explained that the night before in a local bar some jerk had called him a lousy Marine and a Polack, so they had had a tussle. As for myself, there is no way I would call a Marine a lousy person, but I don't know about the Polack thing. I asked this officer how he felt about fighting a war with one hand tied behind his back. His answer told me a lot about the Viet Nam war and its ramifications.

After the tail end of another Viet Nam trip I dropped into a local shopping mall and as I came out of the store I was accosted by a young man who was handing out leaflets. He looked pretty hefty to me, like he could have been an L.A. Rams fullback. He wanted me to support his cause, which was colored people with their problems. I countered with my own cause, and it's Uncle Sugar Able. If Uncle Sam wins, I win also; but if he loses I also lose, so that's my cause. I admitted that I was too old to be standing around street corners passing out leaflets, but could only do what was left for me at my old age by flying jets to the war zone for my cause. After I asked him how he found Viet Nam he said, "I ain't never been to Viet Nam. I'm a college student."

NOTHING good lasts forever, and this ugly word called retirement caught up with me. But I do count my blessings because I was lucky enough to survive the rigors of hood checks, en route checks, and especially those frequent physical examinations, any one of which, if failed, could put an early end to one's career.

My final flight was from Honolulu to San Francisco, arriving at about 3:00 A.M. with an almost empty airplane that was returning from Viet Nam. The crew chief scrambled aboard and asked if I had brought him a good one. I gave him the important news that this was my last flight after thirty-three years with United and that, yes, we had brought him a good one, but he seemed to be only interested in the condition of the plane.

Returning to my home port, Los Angeles, now as a mere passenger, I said so-long to a couple of friends, drove home and entered the nostalgic and sometimes gloomy world out of the mainstream.

In the meantime my boss and another friend arranged a going away party for me and, to my knowledge at the time, the event was to be just a few friends having more than a few drinks and telling even more lies. What a surprise party it turned out to be. A mini-crowd of pilots, copilots, stewardesses and dispatchers showed up, and it was only then that I realized I would not miss the flying per se, but I would most miss these characters with whom I had worked for thirty-three years. I was awarded some trophies and a stereo receiver and a record player and, last but not least, a large framed picture of the last airplane I flew for United. On it were 203 signatures of the people I had worked with. The icing on the cake came after the party when a half-dozen stewardesses invited me out to dinner in Manhattan Beach.

I survived this night and returned home to Santa Barbara intact.

A little adjustment on my part enabled me to now fly a plane from the back seat in the cabin. There I can help the skipper with his landings and can twist and squirm to get him back on the centerline and I can worry for him when we enter a thunderstorm. Also I can select the flights I fly which is a perk I never had while on active status.

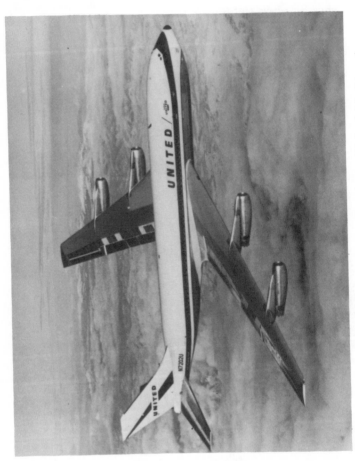

The Douglas DC-8 jet transport. (Photo: United Air Lines.)

Last going-away present at my retirement party,
with 203 signatures including pilots, stewardesses, dispatchers, and crew desk lads.
The DC-8 shown is the one I flew at the tail end of a Saigon trip.

*Above: Tools of the trade before retirement—scintallometer for
uranium prospecting; sabre to be carried when officer
of the day; pilot helmets of the 1930s;
calculator, log, slide rule, and adding machine.
Below: After retirement—woodworking shop where retiree
saws up big boards into little ones.*

CHAPTER 10
Retirement

MY DAUGHTER AND FAMILY moved to Australia, where her husband served as head librarian at a local university. Neither Mary nor I had ever been to this country, and the propaganda that we were fed convinced us that we should pay them a visit, which we did and were not disappointed.

Arriving in Sydney we enjoyed the sights around the city and rolled up a hefty bill at the Wentworth Hotel. When the bill was presented I was informed that my Visa Card carried no weight in Australia. This was quite a shock since I had planned to pay for the entire journey with my Visa, some travelers checks and a little cash. (The plane and train tickets were purchased in advance.) We were bailed out of this mess by some cash infusions from my daughter and her husband. Later my Visa was restored as an acceptable charge account tool in Australia.

A four-hour flight to Alice Springs in the center of Australia was similar to the old airline flights of the 1930s, always JUST OFF THE GROUND in a small aircraft with everyone aboard ended up knowing everyone else and the captain was none other than an attractive young lady. In Alice Springs a tour around the town took us past the house of the very same captain who had flown us in and her residence was the highlight of the tour. I doubt that my quonset hut here in Santa Barbara will ever be on exhibit in any tour around here.

We returned to Melbourne via the old Ghan narrow-gauge railroad, which was a jewel. It had wooden coaches, tiny staterooms and a most congenial crew and other stuff. General Douglas MacArthur made this trip during WWII. The railway was about to be phased out shortly, and we rode one of its last runs.

Rains threatened our arrival in Melbourne on time, and even our arrival at all. When we crossed a bridge over a raging river the tracks squashed up and down with only a few inches of clearance above the water as we went over. But the scenery was there along with the 'roos, emus and quaint railroad stations. At these stations the boarding passengers had their muddy shoes wiped off with a towel by the conductor.

After arriving only a few hours late in Melbourne we were met by my daughter and family with their stationwagon and complete camping gear, and so we took off on a great trip through the grape-and-sheep country and the outback. We even camped on the Darling River, where the cuckoo birds screamed at Mary as she brushed her teeth early each morning—but only for about fifteen minutes, after which everything became quiet.

Along the way in the outback Mary had to go to the restroom, which of necessity turned out to be a local pub for men only, as all Aussie pubs are. She was dressed properly for the outback and looked like someone from another world. After some delay Jim suggested that I go in and see what was going on. In the pub there were a few men who seemed stunned by this apparition that just strolled through. I went back to the relief room and a voice came out saying, "I'll be out in a minute." I would bet an even dollar that those lads are still talking about that one.

A trip to Tasmania wound up this junket with it's gambling casino, rain forests, and the home of the legendary tylacinth, supposedly extinct but with frequent "sightings" even today. On the way back to the airport I was driving my car at the posted speed limit in a long line of cars when two patrolmen pulled me out of the line and said that I was speeding according to their radar. I gave them a tirade about the fact that I had never been cited for speeding in my decades of auto driving and that this was a scam of the first order. They let me off the hook on this violation but were laughing their heads off as we pulled away.

Leaving home again we tried a 'round-the-world venture that took us to Zurich, Switzerland, to Sri Lanka, to Hongkong, Hawaii and back to home base. Plans for the trip included our itinerary and accommodations in Sri Lanka. When we arrived in Colombo we were met at the airport by a government official who gave us a warm welcome, and also a tourist guide who offered us a package deal of 284 American dollars total to replace my original plan for the week. His offer included an auto with a guide driver, a Jeep trip through the southern jungle and accommodations throughout. It was an offer too good to be true, as so we accepted.

The Jeep drive in the jungle afforded us views of elephants, crocodiles and other denizens, and was well worth the price, but there was more to come with the high country, the Kandy Dancers and the tea plantations.

Leaving the high country, we came near the area where the movie *Bridge Over the River Kwai* was filmed. I conned the driver to take us a little off the prescribed route to see the site of this great movie. Walking down to the river, I picked up a leech on my arm and did the wrong thing by yanking it off. At the river a few locals joined up with us and pointed out through our interpreter the key spots of the film's actions. The wooden parts of the bridge were taken away by the natives and used elsewhere. This side trip was well worth the extra thirty-five dollars that the tour man assessed us even though he was upset about our deviation from his original package.

The people of Sri Lanka are very attractive and exceptionally interested in us Americans. They grinned and smiled at us at every turn. At one point several people were gathered around a youth of perhaps thirteen or fourteen and were really dressing him down. Our tour chauffeur told us that the lad had just made an offensive remark to a young girl and he was in big trouble.

On the way home in Hong Kong we received a cable from Mary's sister in Chicago telling us that her dad had passed away. The rest of the trip was under a pall, of course, but we made it home without any further glitches, except for the one in Honolulu when Mary, in her disturbed frame of mind, left a valuable necklace that she had purchased in Hong Kong in the hotel room.

Now that I had become a seasoned back-seat driver with no command authority I selected a more adventurous itinerary for next trip— Siberian Railroad from Moscow to Kosmolosk on the eastern end of Siberia. On our flight to New York to join up with the expedition, a stewardess informed us that a Korean airliner, flight 007, had just been shot down by the Russians and that all aboard were lost. This was not the best way to start such a trip but we continued on to New York to meet the tour leader, who told us that there would be no change in plans and that the trip would go on as scheduled.

When we arrived in Moscow total frustration took over. Endless forms had to be filled out, and long lines seemed to be necessary to get anywhere. At the baggage inspection three pairs of blue jeans which one of our group had brought along for the trip were confiscated because officials said he was going to black market them.

After getting cleared to enter the Soviet Union we were checked into the International Hotel, a luxury abode overlooking the Kremlin and within walking distance of many other sights. Our suite consisted of a living room, a bedroom and a bath, and had a balcony overlooking the Kremlin and the streets below.

In late evening we boarded our train, and the departure was very impressive. Apparently this was a major event for the Moscovites, for there seemed to be a thousand people on hand to see us off. Singers and dancers and a band performed on the station platform as we boarded the train.

Our luxury wheels consisted of two sleeping cars, two dining cars, a club and bar car, a food storage car and a kitchen car. The next few days as we rolled eastward were spent meeting our fellow travelers and trying to fit into our stateroom which turned out to be very comfortable. It was pleasant to watch the little villages go by as well as the great forests and rivers as we crossed the Urals and entered Siberia.

Novosibirsk was the first stop, and here we left the train for a day or two to stay at a hotel and roam the city. We took only a few toilet articles with us, leaving our main luggage aboard the train. The visit included the "think tank" of the USSR and a museum of Siberia's minerals, which must be among the world's largest, including diamonds, rubies, gold, silver, platinum, coal, oil and uranium.

In the evening we had a dinner and dance session. Mary especially enjoyed the evening by being asked to dance with a young man who was suave, charming and eager, according to her. He kissed her hand numerous times and bowed from time to time as all would-be gentlemen should. It turned out that he was a Russian fighter pilot who had just returned from Cuba. As I left the ballroom with Mary he glared at me and I smiled at him.

Back on the train we were railed to Irkutsk on Lake Baikal, which is the largest fresh-water lake in the world, about 400 miles long and a mile deep. The lake has many unusual species of fish and even salt-water seals, although it is not known how they got there. The Siberian tiger once roamed this area around Baikal but is now thought to be extinct. We were shown a small museum on the lake and their research on the flora and fauna of the the region. One specimen of great interest was a transparent fish with its ribs and backbone showing like an X-ray.

We roamed around the tiny villages with their woody houses and tiny gardens which were the best, even in Siberia. At a noon lunch at the one and only restaurant, a glass of water was sitting on the table and I took a generous sip of the stuff. It turned out to be pure vodka.

On leaving Irkutsk I wrangled a visit to the cockpit of our train for two or three hours, and this was a real experience. One of the younger girls on our trip and, of course, the KGB looking over my shoulder, accompanied me to the engineer's cab. The engineer and his copilot were ecstatic although neither of us understood the other. As I snuck aboard the cab two Russian soldiers took notice and chased after the train and me. One of our tour leaders panicked when she couldn't account for my absence in the passenger compartment. The ride in the train was especially interesting since the crews coming from the opposite direction saw in passing a young girl in our crew. There was heavy traffic on this line and much of it was military equipment such as trucks, tanks and artillery.

Then on to the end of the line at Khaborosvk, the eastern end of Siberia. This train venture was similar to an ocean cruise. Activities and entertainment were abundant. We were offered a course in the Russian language which, upon completion, would enable us to do a fair job of understanding the language. I quit after two lessons and Mary after three, and about all I got out of it was *nyet* and *da*. The Russian girl who was our guide spoke perfect English and filled us in on the interesting aspects of our visit. At one point she discussed the downing of the Korean airliner, which she claimed was an American spy plane, but then she suddenly broke down in tears, which terminated that part of the lecture.

Normally one would think of Russia as being short of staples and fresh vegetables which we Americans grow in abundance, but one of our rail cars was full of fresh vegetables that looked as if they had just come out of one of our supermarkets. The chefs had a lot of good stuff to choose from and did their culinary skills on two wood burning stoves and ovens. The daily breads and pastries were as tasty as any in my experience. At one point the train stopped and the chefs got out and gathered some berries along the tracks which they converted into preserves for our next breakfast.

At Khaborosvk, the eastern end of Siberia, we bade goodbye to the train and crew with some reluctance; we were beginning to like this train life. In the evening we attended a delightful cultural performance. The costumes, dancing, and music were spirited and perfectly executed. This was the best performance of any that we attended in all of Russia.

The flight back to Moscow took eight hours, during which we could observe the immensity of Siberian geography. There were thousands of miles of forests, lakes and rivers, but no settlements except for those along the railroad. Back in Moscow we were checked into the same Hotel International and into the same suite that we had stayed in before. The Russian circus was

*Two hours at the helm of the Siberian Express
east of Lake Baikal.*

our entertainment for the evening. The circus was unusual, not at all like American circuses, which include the usual parades, large tents, clowns and trapeze performers, the things we consider a circus. Instead this show was held in a permanent enclosed theater with ornate decorations and trappings and there was no steam calliope or animals in the parade before the circus began.

Between halves the big deal was lining up for ice-cream cones and since Mary was allergic to most animals she went for the ice-cream lineup. I stayed my course and saw the entire show—the performing bears, the trapeze artists and even a few horses. Frankly, I like our own early circuses much better.

The next day we roamed around on our own through Red Square, the Kremlin and other spots. The Gum department store, the largest in Russia, was glass-roofed and had three long rows of shops two levels high, and gave us an insight into the quality of Russian goods. Outside a large bunch of soldiers were practicing for their big parade in November and I asked a policeman if I could photograph the action, and he gave his consent. This was the only time I was able to photograph anything of a military nature.

That evening our group went to a restaurant that served Georgian food but Mary and I went to the Bolshoi Ballet instead. The building was inside the Kremlin and alone was worth the visit. We lucked out on this choice because several of the party were nauseated by the food at the Georgian restaurant.

By now we had received word that several nations had stopped all Aeroflot flights into their countries. The Russians took it out on us with a vengeance. At the checkout for our departure to Leningrad each of us had to have all bags weighed and we were nailed for the excess baggage. The Russian plane was the most uncomfortable craft we had ever encountered. The seats were of the tiniest, and the long wait at the end of the runway put us into a stupor, because the ventilation was nowhere. Some of our passengers felt like passing out, so finally we demanded that the stewardess open the cabin door for a little fresh air. Nevertheless we made it to Leningrad and checked into a hotel on the River Niva where the Aurora cruiser was anchored.

The city turned out to be one of the most magnificent cities of Russia with its Petrodvorets—the summer palace of the czars—and of course the great Hermitage museum.

Another circus was scheduled for the evening but Mary and I were a bit tired so we repaired back to the hotel. After midnight I got a little restless and decided to take a walk around the hotel and across the bridge past the Aurora cruiser. Crossing the bridge I was accosted by three young punks who muttered something about chewing gum. I thought that this was it and that I had just bought the farm, but I brushed them off with a long diatribe in English and they took off like scampering jackanapes. Even Russia has its own street creeps, but I doubt that theirs will ever come up to ours in the USA.

Checking out through Russian customs and immigration we were given the final heave-ho by these artisans of harassment. Long lines, the best of nitpicking, tearing off our baggage claim tags and even taking me aside to be questioned about my gold class ring from the Air Corps Flying School of 1929. I was told that taking gold out of the country was a *nyet-nyet*. Finally, when the wheels left the ground on takeoff, the group let out a cheer that must have been heard clear back to the Kremlin. A stewardess opened the cockpit door so that the flight crew could hear this sitting ovation.

There were other trips in the making such as a canal boat cruise on the Llongathlian canal from Chester, England, to Llongathlian in Wales and return. On this trip I was the skipper and Mary opened and closed the locks and raised the drawbridges along the canal, which is as it should be. We bought a week's supply of food but found out soon enough that it was more enjoyable to go ashore and visit a pub for the evening meal. At the end of the canal boat trip we turned over a bundle of food for the next boaters.

But none of these excursions did much for me as a simple flight as captain with any destination to anywhere while I was working as such. This must mean that I have wound down, and

168 ■   CARL "RECK" RECKNAGEL

I have also noticed recently that the man in the yellow flannel nightgown has been smiling at me and has asked me for my hat size.

Antoine de Saint-Exupery, mentioned before, may have described his own retirement something like this, in his own classic style: "Suddenly a pall of silence rings down the curtain on life's sparkle and the realization penetrates one's mind that one's part in the flow is nary a ripple, the dullest of emotions." Personally I'd rather be working.

The Ending

IN RETROSPECT, HAVING MADE IT from chemical engineer to Air Force officer and airline pilot to retirement, I must consider myself among the more fortunate. Anyone who even makes it to my age in good health has a bundle of good luck going for him.

Although I was trained by the Air Corps in low-altitude combat flying, I was never directly involved in combat during World War II, Viet Nam or Korea, but because of the timing of my age I was relegated to transport flying throughout these wars.

So the little lady called Luck has been kind to me, for which I am grateful.

But as some of the more knowledgeable writers indicate, the most difficult part of any writing is to get it started and to end it. In my case this is true. But, as my four-year-old grandson announced when we were out flying a four-inch balsa airplane, "Pa Pa, you are too old to fly airplanes anymore."

Cockpits through the ages.
Above: The Wright Brothers' flyer had a control stick for rudder and elevator control and a saddle-like affair in which Orville lay prone and wiggled his hips like a belly dancer to warp the wings for lateral control. 1903.
Below: A later cockpit, the B-2 stealth bomber. The control is now a "stick," in the center of the plane, and the plane commander now sits on the right side. The saddle control is no longer needed.

Portrait by my wife, Mary Leppla.